Living Beyond Belief

Group
Loveland, Colorado

LIVING BEYOND BELIEF

Copyright © 1999 Group Publishing, Inc.

All rights reserved. No part of this book may be reproduced in any manner whatsoever without prior written permission from the publisher, except where noted in the text and in the case of brief quotations embodied in critical articles and reviews. For information write Permissions, Group Publishing, Inc., Dept. PD, P.O. Box 481, Loveland, CO 80539.

Credits
Contributing Authors: Tim Baker, Debbie Gowensmith, Dennis R. McLaughlin, Erika Moss
Editor: Amy Simpson
Creative Development Editor: Jim Kochenburger
Chief Creative Officer: Joani Schultz
Copy Editor: Dena Twinem
Art Director and Designer: Jean Bruns
Cover Art Director: Jeff A. Storm
Cover Designer: Rick Dembicki
Computer Graphic Artist: Pat Miller
Illustrator: Marty Norman
Production Manager: Alexander Jorgensen

Unless otherwise noted, Scripture taken from the HOLY BIBLE, NEW INTERNATIONAL VERSION®. Copyright © 1973, 1978, 1984 by International Bible Society. Used by permission of Zondervan Publishing House. All rights reserved.

Library of Congress Cataloging-in-Publication Data
Living beyond belief/ [contributing authors, Tim Baker...et al. ;
  editor, Amy Simpson].
       p.   cm.
     ISBN 0-7644-2099-2 (alk. paper)
     1. Church group work with teenagers. 2. Bible–Study and
  teaching. I. Baker, Tim. II. Simpson Amy.
  BV4447.L497 1999
  268'.433–dc21   99-30359
                                                                         CIP

10 9 8 7 6 5 4 3 2 1   08 07 06 05 04 03 02 01 00 99

Printed in the United States of America.

Contents

INTRODUCTION 4

Holy Interruptions: **ABRAHAM** 6
    God guides us. (Genesis 12:1-5; 13:14-18; 15:1-18)

Divine Astonishment: **SARAH** 12
    God surprises us. (Genesis 18:1-15; 21:1-7)

Stairway to Heaven: **JACOB** 19
    God is with us. (Genesis 28:10-22)

God's Faithfulness in the Headlines: **RUTH** 25
    God provides for us. (Ruth 1–4)

Go to Shiloh: **HANNAH** 32
    God hears our prayers. (1 Samuel 1:1-20)

Nothing Separates Us: **DAVID** 38
    God loves us unconditionally. (2 Samuel 11:1-17, 26–12:17;
    Psalms 32; 51; 103; Romans 8:38-39)

God Speaks: **ELIJAH** 45
    God speaks to us. (1 Kings 19:1-16)

An Unlikely Hero: **ESTHER** 52
    God calls us. (Esther 4:1–5:8; 7:1-6)

The Power of Protection: **DANIEL** 59
    God protects us. (Daniel 6:1-28)

A Fish Story: **JONAH** 66
    God teaches us. (Jonah 1–4)

Canceled Debts: **A SINFUL WOMAN** 73
    God forgives us. (Luke 7:36-50)

Kneel Down: **MARTHA** 81
    God wants us to know him. (Luke 10:38-42)

Come Down From Your Tree: **ZACCHAEUS** 87
    God changes us. (Luke 19:1-10)

Introduction

So your teenagers have been to Sunday school, many of them for years. They've attended countless events, meetings, prayer groups, and concerts. They say all the right things and live good, moral lives. A few of them even seem to know the Bible better than you do.

But do they really know God? Sure, they've met God, but have they experienced God in a real, life-changing way? Your teenagers are hungry for encounters with God that will bring meaning to their lives and to their study of Scripture.

Give them a life-changing experience with God in these thirteen Bible studies designed to help your young people know God better. Each Bible study in *Living Beyond Belief* helps students understand the way God was powerfully present in the life of a biblical man or woman. And your youth will participate in active and interactive learning experiences to recognize the same attributes of God in their own lives.

Because your youth need to build personal relationships with God—not just learn about God—each Bible study includes a worship experience designed to help them respond directly to God. And because all your young people are unique, these Bible studies use a variety of learning styles to help different types of learners have authentic experiences with God.

As you prepare each Bible study, be sure to check out the "Bible Background" boxes. These boxes will provide you with interesting cultural and historical context you may want to share with your students to help them understand Bible events.

Use the in-depth Bible studies in this book to help your students apply the Bible to their own lives and truly experience God. You'll be helping to build in them a solid foundation for the future: knowing and loving God.

13 Relational Bible Studies

Holy Interruptions

BIBLE CHARACTER: ABRAHAM

SCRIPTURE: Genesis 12:1-5; 13:14-18; 15:1-18

THEME:
God guides us.

SUPPLIES:
You'll need masking tape, string, a pen or pencil, index cards, Bibles, photocopies of the "Weaving Into God's Guidance" handout (p. 11), pencils, soft instrumental music, a cassette or CD player, newsprint, markers, and three clothespins for each person.

PREPARATION

Before the session, place a line of masking tape on the floor in your meeting area. Use the tape to map out an indirect route from one end of your meeting area to the other. Find another adult to help you lead groups to their starting places.

Hang a piece of string across your meeting area. Write the following words on three separate index cards, and tape them at equal intervals along the string: "I need to listen more," "I need to know God better," and "I need to be ready to follow God." Make one photocopy of the "Weaving Into God's Guidance" handout (p. 11) for each person.

Study Genesis 12:1-5; 13:14-18; and 15:1-18. Then read the entire session outline. Make sure all the activities fit your group, and make any necessary changes.

OVERVIEW

This session teaches students about Abraham's experience with God. It helps students understand that God guides us

6

through all phases of our lives. Students will
- experience what it's sometimes like to search for God's guidance,
- study how Abraham found and followed God's guidance,
- work through some principles for following God's guidance, and
- apply those principles to their lives through reflective worship.

OPENER

As students arrive, have them gather in a location outside your meeting area, such as a hallway or a room adjacent to your meeting area. When everyone has arrived, inform students that they'll be going on a "blind" trip. Have students form two groups and close their eyes. Have group members link arms, and lead the groups into your meeting area. Lead one group to the beginning of the tape line you've laid out. Lead the other group to a location beside the first group. Have both groups keep their eyes shut.

When groups are at their locations, have group members unlink their arms. Say: **You're about to take an unusual kind of trip. On the floor is a marker that will direct you on your path. Keeping your eyes shut, I'd like each group to work together to find your path and follow it. You can try anything to find your path—get down on hands and knees or take off your shoes, for example.**

Have groups keep their eyes shut and begin searching for the path. Allow groups two minutes to try to follow the path. When time is up, call groups together and ask:
- **How did it feel to search for the path?**
- **How did you feel when you couldn't find the path?**
- **How did you feel when you did find the path?**
- **In this activity, did it make a difference which group you were in? Explain.**
- **Was it a challenge to keep your eyes closed as you were searching?**
- **How is this activity like the way we sometimes pursue God's guidance in our lives? How is it different?**

BIBLE BACKGROUND

You may want to share this background information with your students to help them understand the story of Abraham.

God's call on Abraham's life was intended to try his faith and obedience and to set him apart for God. God's call tested Abraham's devotion. Abraham had to choose whether he loved his native soil or he was willing to leave it and follow God's call. Once Abraham did follow God's call, he became set apart—God's chosen man for a huge responsibility and a lifelong challenge.

BIBLE BACKGROUND

You may want to share this background information with your students to help them understand the story of Abraham.

Ur, the land Abraham left, is rich in history. It was named for the Chaldeans, the people who settled there around 900 B.C. Ur of the Chaldeans was the principle center for worship of the Sumerian moon god Nanna. It's possible that Abraham was never exposed to the worship of God until God spoke to him.

Ur was a town with a complex system of government and a well-developed system of commerce. There were town drains, two-story houses, and a great temple tower. Abraham was leaving a well-developed, comfortable society when he set out on his journey.

• How does God guide us?
• Do you think we need God's guidance? Why or why not?

UNDERSTANDING GOD'S WORD

Say: Sometimes trying to understand where God is guiding us can feel like we're searching with our eyes shut, or even looking for something we'll never find. But it doesn't have to be that way. Today we're going to learn about a guy who wasn't on a search to find God's will; he simply was open to God's guidance when God spoke to him. He learned that God's guidance spans throughout the lives of people who trust him.

Remind students about the story of Abraham. Explain that God promised to make Abraham a great nation, to bless him, and to bless all people through him. That was an awesome statement, considering Abraham was about seventy-five years old. Have students form three groups, and assign each group one of these passages to read: Genesis 12:1-5; 13:14-18; and 15:1-18. Then have the three groups work together to retell the story of Abraham in their own words.

Have students form groups of four. Ask the following questions, giving groups time to discuss each question before you ask the next one:

• Why do you think God chose to reveal the plan to Abraham in the way he did?

• What's the significance of what God said to Abraham in Genesis 15:1-18?

• Why didn't Abraham disobey God and decide to follow his own plan?

• What does Abraham's life reveal about God's guidance in our lives?

• How do people who don't know God search for guidance in their lives?

• When we think God is guiding us, how can we be sure it's coming from God?

Conclude the discussion by asking students who are sure of God's guidance in their lives to share how they've discovered God's plans for them. Discuss the various ways God might communicate and convince people of his guidance. Use the life of Abraham as an example as you lead students to a more personal understanding of God's guidance.

APPLYING GOD'S WORD

Say: **Sometimes people feel like it's impossible to try to understand God's guidance for our lives. Many times we wait, only to come up empty. The key is in understanding why, how, and when God guides us.**

Have students form four groups. Give each person a photocopy of the "Weaving Into God's Guidance" handout (p. 11) and a pencil. Have group members work on their own to complete their handouts and then discuss their answers with the rest of their group.

When groups have answered the questions, have them share their responses with the rest of the class. Then ask:

• **What struggles do you face as you attempt to follow God's guidance?**

• **How do you know that following God's guidance is worthwhile? Explain.**

• **Of the three areas on your handout, what is your greatest area of weakness? Explain.**

• **What are some general ways God guides us?**

• **How can we be sure we're sensing God's guidance and not something else?**

• **How can we "turn up the volume" of God's voice of guidance in our lives?**

WORSHIP TIME

Say: **Now let's spend some time worshipping God for providing guidance in our lives. As I play some music, think about some of the ways God has provided guidance in your life.**

BIBLE BACKGROUND

You may want to share this background information with your students to help them understand the story of Abraham.

It's easy to think that Abraham went out on an uncharted journey and traveled a route no one had ever taken. Actually, that's not the case. God's instructions to Abraham weren't nearly so mysterious as we often think. The trade route from Ur to Haran was a well-traveled route. In fact, there were routes that extended well beyond these two cities. And since the rainfall was regular and plentiful, Abraham's large number of animals would have been well fed on the journey.

Have students sit in their groups with their heads bowed and their eyes closed. Play a quiet, reflective instrumental song for them. When the song is over, have students share some of the things that came to their minds as they listened.

Then give each group a sheet of newsprint and a marker. Have each group write lyrics to the song that praise God for guiding them. Encourage groups to focus on praising God in their songs.

When groups are finished, have groups take turns leading the other groups in worship through the songs they wrote.

CLOSING

Give each person three clothespins and one marker. Have students mark their clothespins with their own identifying marks and number them one through three. When students are finished, point out the string hanging across your meeting area, and read aloud the pieces of paper taped to the string. Have teenagers rate themselves on their ability in each of the three areas by placing their number one clothespin on the area they need to work on the most, then their second clothespin on the area they'd like to work on second, and their third clothespin on the remaining area.

Point out to students that we're all in different places in our ability to trust God's guidance. Reassure them that God guides each of us differently—in different directions and in different ways.

Have students form groups based on the areas they'd like to work on first. With students in their groups, have them share why they feel the area they've chosen is the primary area they want to work on. When everyone has had a chance to share, have group members pray for one another. Then have students form groups based on their second choices and repeat the activity.

When groups have shared and prayed, close the meeting in prayer, thanking God for guidance and for the ability to follow God as Abraham did.

Weaving Into God's Guidance

Knowing How

So God guides us. And to sense God's guidance, you've got to know God and be willing to follow. But there's another important aspect: You've got to know *how* God guides us. How do you find out? You've got some research to do.

First read about people in the Bible who followed God's guidance. How did they experience God's guidance? What means did God use to guide them?

Second, talk to others who have followed God's guidance. Meet with your pastor. Ask someone you respect to share with you how God has guided that person.

Then look for ways God might be guiding you. Will you hear God's voice? Will God speak to you in a dream? Will you feel a gentle leading? Know how God has led others, and you'll be closer to knowing how God might lead you.

Paying Attention: Use these questions to guide you as you consider how God might lead you:

- Who can you talk to so you can know more about God's guidance?
- What Bible passages can you look through to understand more about God's guidance?
- How have you sensed God's guidance in the past? How have you responded?

Relationship With God

A *huge* part of God's guidance in our lives comes through our relationship with God—our regular contact with God. God not only *loves* it when we spend time with him, but the time we spend also deepens our relationship with God and opens up the lines of communication for God to lead us.

Our relationship with God is key to knowing where God is guiding. Consider this: If we pursue God only to get guidance, we'll begin to see God only as someone who coldly directs our lives. But if we pursue a strong relationship with God, that guidance bursts out of a thriving, warm connection with the Almighty. And we'll recognize God's voice like we do the voice of an old friend rather than a drill sergeant.

Beefing Up: Use these questions to guide you as you consider your relationship with God:

- What do you need to do to know God better?
- How can you make a stronger connection with God?
- What pictures come to mind when you think of God?
- On a scale from 1 to 10, how would you rate your trust in God's guidance?

Willingness to Follow

Look at the life of Abraham, and you'll see one thing very clearly—this was a man who asked "How high?" when God said "Jump!" Abraham's choice to follow God's guidance demonstrates how God wants us to live our lives. We have to be ready to hear God's voice. And we must be willing to take action when God asks us to.

Following Closely: Use these questions to guide you as you consider your response to God's guidance:

- Are you willing to go wherever God leads? How do you know whether you're willing?
- Are you scared of doing whatever God asks? What can you do to get more confident?

Divine Astonishment

SARAH

BIBLE CHARACTER:

SCRIPTURE: Genesis 18:1-15; 21:1-7

THEME:
God surprises us.

SUPPLIES:
You'll need photocopies of the "Dissecting a Surprise" handout (p. 17) and the "Surprising Prayers" handout (p. 18), Bibles, paper, pencils or pens, and modeling clay.

PREPARATION

Before the session, prepare your meeting area so you can darken it during the meeting. Make one photocopy of the "Dissecting a Surprise" handout (p. 17) and one photocopy of the "Surprising Prayers" handout (p. 18) for each person.

Read Genesis 18:1-15; 21:1-7. Then read the entire session outline. Make sure that all the activities fit your group, and make any necessary changes.

OVERVIEW

This session teaches students about Sarah's experience with God. It helps students understand how and why God surprises us. This session also helps students discover what surprises are and how they might look for surprises in their daily experience with God. Students will

- experience a surprise and analyze it,
- study the story of Sarah and the surprise God gave her,
- re-create an experience of receiving a surprise from God,

- respond in worship to what they learn about God's surprises, and
- pray about surprises they'd like to receive from God.

OPENER

Before students arrive, find something in your meeting room you can hide behind, and completely hide yourself. As students arrive, jump out of your hiding place and yell "Surprise!" Then have students join you in surprising other students as they arrive. When everyone has arrived, ask:

- **How did you feel about the way you were welcomed?**

Have students form four groups, and ask each group to meet in a different corner of the room. Encourage each group to devise a way to surprise another group. For example, a group might try to sneak up on another group, bring another group treats if you have snacks available, or sing "Happy Birthday" to another group. Once groups have their surprises prepared, turn off the lights and give groups time to find and surprise each other.

When groups have surprised each other, turn on the lights and ask:

- **What are the essential ingredients in a surprise?**
- **When have you been surprised?**
- **How do you feel about surprises?**
- **Have you ever been surprised by God? Explain.**
- **What are some ways God surprises people?**

UNDERSTANDING GOD'S WORD

Say: **Of all the things you know about God, I'll bet you haven't thought a lot about the ways God loves to surprise us. Just when we least expect it, and when we really need it, God often does things that totally catch us off guard. Today we're going to look deeper into God's surprises by studying the life of Sarah, whom God surprised in a most unusual way.**

BIBLE BACKGROUND

You may want to share this background information with your students to help them understand the story of Sarah.

The three visitors in this story have been the focus of much theological questioning. Who were these three people? Many commentators suggest that two of the men were angels (Genesis 19:1). And because of Abraham's demeanor and the way he addresses the third man, the other man is thought to be God himself. Imagine not only being surprised by God, but getting that surprise in person!

Remind students of the story of Sarah, Abraham's wife. Explain that Sarah was nearly ninety years old when God told her she was going to have a baby. Have students form groups of three and read Genesis 18:1-15. When groups are finished reading, give each person a piece of paper and a pencil or pen. Say: **I'd like you to imagine for a moment that you're Sarah or some other character in this story. For example, you could imagine you're Sarah's husband, Abraham. Or you might imagine you're one of the visitors, a servant, or a camel. Spend the next thirty seconds thinking about what that experience might have been like for the character you imagine yourself to be. Then write a description of the experience from that character's point of view. Consider what you would have seen, smelled, heard, felt, said, and thought during that experience.**

Give students several minutes to write their descriptions, then ask students to read their descriptions aloud for the other people in their groups.

Next have students read Genesis 21:1-7 in their groups. When they're finished reading, say: **Great job. Now time has passed and Sarah has had her baby. Imagine that Sarah is attending a conference, and they've asked her to share her story with the other people at the conference. Create a speech that Sarah might give to the gathering.**

Have the people in each group work together to serve as Sarah's speech writers. When groups have created their speeches, have someone from each group present the group's speech to everyone else. When all groups have presented, ask:

• Why was God concerned about giving Sarah a child?

• Why do you think God didn't give Sarah a child much earlier?

• Why did Sarah laugh? What was significant about her laughing?

• What do you think God might teach you through Sarah's experience?

• How would you react if God surprised you like this? Explain.

Say: **One thing's for sure—being surprised like this will make** you think. **And it might change the way you live.** Then ask:

• **If you were surprised like this, how would it affect the way you live?**

• **If God surprised you like this, how would it change your understanding of God?**

APPLYING GOD'S WORD

Say: **Getting a big surprise from God is neat—and God does more than just give babies to surprise us. In fact, God surprises people in many ways. Let's look more closely at what it might be like when God surprises us.**

Have students form four groups. Give each person a "Dissecting a Surprise" handout (p. 17). Assign each group one of the sections on the handout. Have students in each group work together to read through their section of the handout and discuss the questions. When they're finished, have groups present their responses on their handouts to the rest of the class. When all groups have presented, ask:

• **How are these surprises like the surprise God gave Sarah?**

• **Is there a "correct" or "incorrect" way to respond to a surprise from God? Explain.**

• **What have you discovered about God's surprises through this activity? Explain.**

WORSHIP TIME

Say: **Now let's take this opportunity to respond in worship to what we've learned about God's surprises.**

Give everyone a photocopy of the "Surprising Prayers" handout (p. 18) and a pen or pencil. Have students follow the directions on their handouts for completing the worship time.

CLOSING

Say: **Sarah's surprise portrays a neat attribute of God—God loves to surprise us. God loves to do the unexpected. In Sarah's**

BIBLE BACKGROUND

You may want to share this background information with your students to help them understand the story of Sarah.

The hospitality Abraham showed the visitors was typical of his time and culture. One commentary notes these culturally distinctive ways Abraham behaved:

1. Abraham gave prompt attention to his guests.

2. He bowed low to the ground.

3. He addressed one of his guests as "my lord" and called himself "your servant."

4. He acted as if the visitors did him a favor by allowing him to serve them.

5. He asked for water to wash their feet.

6. He prepared a lavish meal for them.

7. He stood nearby, assuming the posture of a servant, to meet their every wish.

(Kenneth Barker, ed., et al., The NIV Study Bible)

life, God did the unexpected by giving her a child. That surprise not only changed her life, but it also changed our lives. Her child became one of the ancestors of Jesus when he was born on earth.

God has various reasons for surprising us. Sometimes it might be to fulfill God's will. Other times it might be to remind us of God's love. And sometimes God surprises us to touch the life of someone else. Whatever the reason, God wants to surprise us. So think for a moment about one surprise you'd love to get from God.

Have students think about one surprise they'd like to get. After several seconds, distribute modeling clay and have students create symbols of the surprises they're looking for. For example, a student may create a dollar sign to symbolize a need for money, a bed to symbolize a period of rest, or a strong tree to symbolize physical healing. After students have made their symbols, have them share the symbols with the rest of the class. When students have shared, ask:

• How are you going to be looking for this surprise?

• What have you learned today that will help you recognize this surprise if it happens?

• How can we help each other understand the surprises God gives us?

Say: Surprises are wonderful. God's surprises are exactly what we need. Let's spend time praying that we'll be ready for God's surprises when they come.

Close the session in prayer.

Dissecting a Surprise

Sarah's experience with God might have been the first recorded surprise God pulled off, but it certainly wasn't the last one God did. Through the following four stages, you're going to illustrate what it might be like to receive a surprise from God.

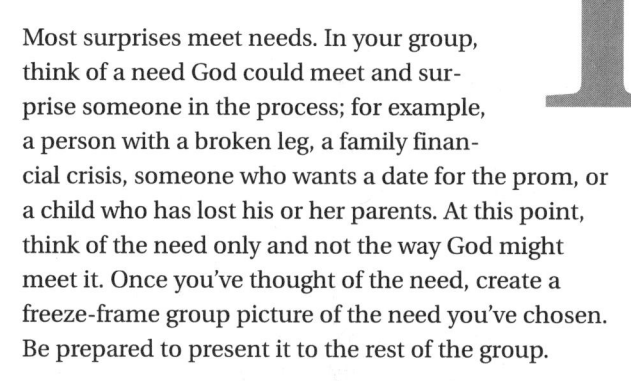

STAGE 1: The Need

Most surprises meet needs. In your group, think of a need God could meet and surprise someone in the process; for example, a person with a broken leg, a family financial crisis, someone who wants a date for the prom, or a child who has lost his or her parents. At this point, think of the need only and not the way God might meet it. Once you've thought of the need, create a freeze-frame group picture of the need you've chosen. Be prepared to present it to the rest of the group.

When you're finished, answer the following questions:

- Are there some needs God wouldn't meet with a surprise? Explain.
- How do God's surprises fit into God's plans for us?
- Is it selfish to tell God the things you'd like to be surprised about? Explain.
- What are some surprises that might not result from needs?

STAGE 2: The Act

A surprise is an action. It's something God does in our physical world. Now come up with two ways to meet a need someone might have. One of the ways must not involve God meeting the need. The other way must involve God meeting the need in a surprising way. Be prepared to share these with the rest of the group.

When you're finished, answer the following questions:

- Which way of meeting the need would you be most likely to rely on? Explain.
- What's the difference between an ordinary surprise and a surprise from God?
- Why do you think God likes to surprise us? Explain.

STAGE 3: The Reaction

Every surprise has a reaction. Consider how a person might react to receiving a surprise from God. Reactions might include disbelief, laughter, anger, or cynicism. Once you've thought through the reaction, create a sixty-second skit that portrays the reaction. Be prepared to share this with the rest of the group.

When you're finished, answer the following questions:

- What's an appropriate way to respond to God's surprises?
- How do you think God wants us react to his surprises? Explain.

STAGE 4: The Proclamation

When we realize we've been surprised, we'll probably want to tell other people about the surprise. Make a list of the people you might tell about a surprise you received from God and the way you might tell them. Be prepared to share your list with the rest of the group.

When you're finished, answer the following questions:

- What are some various ways we can tell others about the surprises God gives us?
- How can you tell others about a surprise if you don't totally understand what God is doing?
- Are there times when it might be best not to tell other people about a surprise from God? Explain.

Surprising Prayers

✏️ **Find two other people** to form a group of three. In your group, pray for someone you feel needs a surprise from God. After you've prayed, write down some of the things you heard others pray about.

✏️ **Find another person** and talk with your partner about some of the things that might prevent you from realizing that God is surprising you. For example, you might be too busy or self-centered. After you and your partner have shared, pray together that God would remove the obstacles. In the space provided, write down some of the things you talked about with your partner.

✏️ **Find two other people** to form a group of three. Tell your partners about a surprise you've received from God. After everyone has had a chance to share, spend time thanking God for giving you surprises. Write about some of the surprises in the space below.

Stairway to Heaven

BIBLE CHARACTER: Jacob

SCRIPTURE: *Genesis 28:10-22*

THEME:
God is with us.

SUPPLIES:
You'll need a videotape with footage of someone surfing very large waves and a VCR (or access to the beach), an object that reminds you of an experience with God, drawing paper, colored pencils, Bibles, a dry-erase board or newsprint and a marker, paper, pens or pencils, offering plates or baskets, soft worship music, a CD or cassette player, chocolate chip cookies, milk, and cups.

PREPARATION

Before the session, if you have access to a beach, arrange for transportation to hold this Bible study session at the beach. If you aren't near a beach or you decide not to take the time to go to a beach, rent a surfing video and cue it to a scene that shows someone surfing very large waves. A popular surfing video is *Endless Summer*, but nearly any surfing video will work because most show large waves.

Take time to think about an experience you've had with God and an object that reminds you of that experience. Try to think of an experience that is concrete and tangible and something your students can relate to. For example, an experience when you felt God's love, faithfulness, or mercy through another person would be great. Find an object that represents your experience, and bring it to the study to show as an example.

Study Genesis 28:10-22. Then read the entire session outline. Make sure all the activities fit your group, and make any necessary changes.

BIBLE BACKGROUND

You may want to share this background information with the students to help them gain insight into the story of Jacob.

Jacob left his home and family due to a family quarrel (Genesis 27:41-43). Jacob was running for his life because his brother wanted to kill him; he had just lied to his father. Jacob probably felt guilty, but he also may have felt intense loss because he wouldn't be able to remain close to his family. He must have felt very lonely. He may have felt uncertain about his future: where he would live, whether he would find a wife, where he would find friends, how he would make a living.

It might have been hard for Jacob to believe God would take care of him. He had no home and no clear future. Then Jacob arrived in Bethel. There God spoke to him in a dream. This may have been the first time Jacob had his own experience with God. Possibly for the first time, he worshipped God and entered into an active relationship with God.

Until this point, Jacob probably had only heard about God from his relatives. When God first spoke to Jacob, he said

continued on page 21

OVERVIEW

This study teaches students to be more aware of God's presence. They'll realize that God is aware of our struggles and is capable of meeting our needs in those struggles. When God meets our deepest needs, we're able to serve God more courageously. Students will

• study how God provided for Jacob during a hard time in his life,

• gain a new perspective on why and how to revere God,

• plan to make a memorial of an experience they've had with God,

• worship God through sacrifice, and

• understand how God satisfies their needs.

OPENER

Have students form groups of three to five people. Give each student a piece of drawing paper. Give each group several colored pencils. Have each group read Genesis 28:10-13 aloud, and instruct each student to draw his or her interpretation of the passage. Encourage students to be creative.

When students are finished drawing, ask:

• **Have you ever had a dream or another experience in which you felt God had spoken to you?**

Allow several students to share their dreams.

• **What are some other ways God reveals himself to us?**

• **Why do you think God revealed a glimpse of heaven to Jacob?**

• **Why do you think God reveals glimpses of heaven to us?**

Allow a few minutes for students to share their drawings with one another, then say: **The stairway Jacob saw in his dream was symbolic of our way to heaven. In John 1:51, Jesus called himself the stairway. A relationship with Jesus is the way for us to get to heaven. The stairway was a symbol of Jesus' role in our lives.**

continued from page 20

(verse 13): "I am…the God of your father Abraham and the God of Isaac." God was identifying himself as the God of Jacob's father and grandfather. As the God of people, not a sun god or a god that represented a concept like love or hate. This identification was part of God's invitation to Jacob to accept the personal God.

Abraham means "father of a multitude." Eventually Jacob's name would be added to the list and God would say, "I am the God of Abraham, Isaac, and Jacob" because Jacob would accept God as his God. Through his life, Jacob would help to fulfill the prophecy that Abraham would be the father of a multitude of people—God's people.

UNDERSTANDING GOD'S WORD

Say: **God gave Jacob a powerful vision of heaven and Jacob's future. Through his dream, Jacob met a personal God and was strengthened in the midst of his struggles.** Have several students read Genesis 28:10-22 aloud, a verse at a time.

Have students discuss the following questions:

• **In your own words, how would you describe Jacob's struggles?**

• **Why do you think God told Jacob about his future?**

• **How would you feel if you were visited by God in such a spectacular way and received a vision from God? Why?**

• **How would you have responded if you were Jacob?**

• **In what specific ways did God reveal himself to Jacob or show Jacob God was with him?**

• **How does God reveal himself to us today?**

APPLYING GOD'S WORD

Say: **After Jacob experienced God, he responded to God in several ways. First he acknowledged God's presence and expressed reverence for God. In verse 16 Jacob said, "Surely the Lord is in this place and I was not aware of it." And verse 17 says he was afraid. To "fear the Lord" means to have respect and an awareness of God's power. Jacob had a healthy "fear of the Lord." It's hard for us to revere God when we don't understand what it means to "fear God." Let's explore this idea further.**

If you're meeting at the beach, point out the waves as they come up on shore. If not, show a video clip of people surfing large waves. Allow the students to watch the power of the waves for about five minutes. Then turn off the video, and point out that the waves are symbolic of God's character.

Ask students to think of similarities between God and the waves. For example, the power of a wave should produce a healthy fear and respect for it. As students call out suggestions,

BIBLE BACKGROUND

Through this amazing vision, God met Jacob at his point of deepest need, and Jacob responded in worship:

• Jacob acknowledged God and expressed a deep reverence for God.

• Jacob set up a pillar and poured oil over it. The pillar and the oil served to remind Jacob of God's character and what God had done at Bethel.

• Jacob named the special place "Bethel," which means "house of God." From that point on, the Israelites would view that place as a holy place, where God could be seen.

• Jacob made a vow that the Lord would be his God. This vow was an act of worship because God had made a promise to Jacob and Jacob responded by making a promise to love God and be devoted to God.

• Jacob promised to give back to God a tenth of all he would receive from the Lord. By doing this, Jacob was acknowledging his dependence on God and expressing his voluntary love. Giving 10 percent of one's income was not yet a commandment (Leviticus 27:30).

---

write the suggestions on a dry-erase board or a piece of newsprint. Then ask:

• **How can we increase our reverence for God?**

• **What are ways we can express reverence for God daily?**

• **How would having more reverence for God change your life?**

Say: **After Jacob's experience with God, he set up a stone as a memorial and anointed it with oil. He also named the place Bethel. These actions were reminders to Jacob and all the Israelites of what God had done there. Think of a time when you experienced God. For example, your experience with God may have come when you became a Christian. Or maybe you've experienced God when you were hiking and enjoying God's beautiful creation.**

After allowing a few minutes for students to think of experiences with God, have each person think of an object that can represent that memory. For example, perhaps a student has a souvenir from a missions trip or a pressed flower from a nature hike. As a model, show them your object and tell the story of your experience with God.

Allow several students to share about their experiences and the objects that can remind them of those experiences with God. If some students can't think of experiences with God, encourage them to wait in expectation for a time when God will meet them in a special way and they can make a memorial.

Encourage students to create memorials of their experiences with God in the future, setting aside those objects as sacred reminders of ways God has been revealed to them. For example, a fallen leaf can remind a student of an experience with God while hiking. A pair of sunglasses could serve as a memorial for an experience with God on a missions trip. A church bulletin can remind someone of an experience with God during a church service. Remind students not to worship the memorials but to use them as reminders to worship God and to have hope when they doubt God.

WORSHIP TIME

Say: **After Jacob created his memorial, he made a vow to serve God and promised to tithe in the future (to give 10 percent of his income back to God). Promising our service and giving our treasures to God are acts of worship. They help us devote our hearts to God and express our dependence on God. They're ways of acknowledging God's goodness and abundance in our lives.**

Give each person paper and a pen or pencil, and have students spend about ten minutes by themselves, writing prayers of thanks to God and acknowledging all the ways God is with them. Encourage students to include in their prayers ways they'll serve God in the future. Suggest that students begin their prayers with these words: "Dear God, thank you for the ways you've been with me throughout my life. You've given me so many glimpses of you..."

Then bring the students back together and take an offering that will go to either a scholarship fund for your group or an organization that needs money. During this worship time, play some soft worship music to help set the mood.

CLOSING

Say: **Jacob had some very specific and deep needs. He was dissatisfied with the mistakes he had made in his past. He was dissatisfied with being homeless. He was dissatisfied with the direction of his life, and God entered the picture and satisfied Jacob's greatest needs. God meets our needs also.**

Give each person two or three chocolate chip cookies. As they're finishing their cookies and probably are getting thirsty, ask:
- How does your mouth feel right now?
- How did the cookies create a need for you?
- What would help satisfy your mouth's need right now?

Give each person a cup of milk to drink. Then ask:
- How is God like milk in our lives?

Say: **We all have deep needs: to feel loved, to be cared for, to** feel safe, to be hopeful about the future, and so on. God created us with those needs, and God wants to meet those needs, even in ways we don't expect. God showed Jacob he was with him during one of the hardest parts of Jacob's life. Jacob felt God's love and responded to it. His life was changed. Throughout your day tomorrow, try to be aware of how God is with you and taking care of you. Then respond to God's presence as Jacob did.

God's Faithfulness in the Headlines

BIBLE CHARACTER:

SCRIPTURE: *Ruth 1–4*

THEME:
God provides for us.

SUPPLIES:
You'll need photocopies of the "Feelings of a Stranger" handout (p. 31), pens or pencils, Bibles, markers, newsprint, paper, two or three weeks worth of whole newspapers, scissors (one pair per person), glue sticks, and tape or tacks.

PREPARATION

Before the session, make one photocopy of the "Feelings of a Stranger" handout (p. 31) for each person. Place the supplies on a common table so all participants have access to them.

Familiarize yourself with the story of Ruth (four chapters). Then read the entire session outline. Make sure all the activities fit your group, and make any necessary changes.

OVERVIEW

The book of Ruth is a short, simple story about God's grace and how God is at work in the world. God provides for us even in the midst of our most difficult circumstances. As part of this lesson, teenagers will create a collage like newspaper that will report on various examples of God providing for people. In this session students will

• discover encouragement in their own lives through the story of Ruth;

• identify how God's grace is at work in the world, though not always in dramatic ways;

- understand that God provides for them in many different ways, including through other people;
- identify people in their lives God uses to provide for them; and
- be challenged to be active in God's care for others.

OPENER

Give each participant a copy of the "Feelings of a Stranger" handout and a pen or pencil. Say: **Most of us know what it feels like to be a stranger in an unfamiliar place. At one time or another, you've probably had to be in a place where you didn't know anyone—whether it was a party, a new school, or a new church. Take a moment to think of a time when you were a stranger in a group. Then use your artistic skills to illustrate how you felt in the situation: On the handout I've given you, draw facial expressions to answer the questions based on your memory of the event. Were you scared? happy? nervous? energized? Were you having a bad hair day? a disgusting zit day? Take about five minutes to think of a situation and draw your feelings.**

After everyone has had an opportunity to complete the handout, have participants form groups of three or four and share their drawings with each other and discuss their experiences. (If you have a group of ten or less, you may want to keep everyone together as a group and allow participants to share with everyone.)

UNDERSTANDING GOD'S WORD

Say: **For most of us, going into a new situation where we don't know anyone can be a source of great anxiety and even fear. Imagine for a moment what it would be like to give up a whole way of life and move to a different country where you didn't know anyone at all. Imagine for a moment leaving your family and moving to a place where everyone spoke a different language and had an entirely different religion.**

BIBLE BACKGROUND

You may want to share this background information with your students to help them understand the story of Ruth.

Widows such as Ruth and Naomi had little to look forward to except difficult times. That was, unless a relative would agree to take responsibility for the extended family. To preserve the family line and the family land, a relative was permitted by Old Testament law (Deuteronomy 25:5-10) to marry the widow. This person was called a "kinsman-redeemer." If no one chose to help the widow, she most likely would live in poverty for the rest of her life because any inheritance would be passed on to the son or nearest male relative. Boaz demonstrated his kindness and generosity as a kinsman-redeemer by marrying Ruth.

This describes what happened to a young woman in the Bible named Ruth. The book of Ruth is a wonderful story of how God provides for those who are in lonely, difficult, and unsure circumstances.

Ask a volunteer to summarize the story of Ruth. If no one is able or willing, provide the group with a brief overview of the events yourself.

Next, have participants form four groups. Assign each group one of the four chapters of Ruth. Give each group a marker and a piece of newsprint.

Say: **Your assignment as a group is to read through your chapter and identify as many examples as you can of God providing for people's needs. When you find an example, record it on your piece of newsprint. The only catch is you have to write it as if it's a newspaper headline. For example, if you see God providing for Ruth when Boaz agrees to marry her, you might record the headline "Boaz Marries Ruth." Continue recording examples until you have completely examined your chapter. You'll have approximately ten minutes to do this.**

After about ten minutes, have a representative from each group give a quick summary of the chapter and share the group's headlines that describe examples of God's provisions. Make sure the groups hang on to their headline sheets because they'll need them later.

After each group has had an opportunity to share, say: **One of the interesting things you may have noticed in the book of Ruth is that God isn't mentioned very often. Even so, God's presence is obvious in many ways. The story of Ruth reminds us that God doesn't always work in our lives in ways that are dramatic. Think for a moment about the birth of Christ. Even though he was a king, God chose a very unusual place for him to be born. No one in Bethlehem was even aware that the Messiah had been born until the shepherds showed up. God could have chosen a fabulous palace for his son to be born in. He could have had angels announce the fact with trumpets. But instead he chose the quiet, out-of-the way place of Bethlehem. God could have chosen to** work very dramatically in the life of Ruth. But instead God chose to work quietly through Ruth. In fact, he even allowed Ruth to become a beggar. As a result, she had to go into the field to pick up the leftover crops.

Ask:
- What generally has been your view of beggars?
- How does the story of Ruth challenge your view of beggars?
- Do you think if you were in the same circumstances as Ruth you could do what she did? Why or why not?
- What does the story of Ruth teach you about how God provides for his people?
- Who do you most admire in the story of Ruth, and why?
- What hope does your group's chapter provide for your life?

Lead the group in a brainstorming session, challenging the teenagers to come up with all the examples they can think of which describe how God provides for people. Record their ideas on a blank sheet of newsprint.

APPLYING GOD'S WORD

Give each participant a sheet of paper, and make pens, pencils, and markers available to everyone.

Say: **Spend the next few minutes in a time of quiet reflection and journaling. The object is to identify ways God has provided for you in your life. You can make a list, write a descriptive paragraph, or draw a picture.**

It's up to you. Whatever you decide, please start with another newspaper headline at the top of your page, such as "God Provides for Katie," or "By God's Grace Alex Survives." Choose a headline that is as simple or as creative as you like, but be sure it describes how God has provided for you. Keep in mind that your journaling article will be seen by others later in the study. Take about ten minutes for this activity.

After teenagers have finished their journaling, say: **The story of Ruth took place in a time of violence, wickedness, and disobedience to God. But to read it you really wouldn't know that God's people were in a time of crisis. Ruth's story shows us that** no matter how discouraging things seem around us, God uses people like Boaz to provide for and take care of those he loves. Take today for example. It seems that whenever you pick up a newspaper, it's full of stories of sadness, violence, and crime. But if you search through the stories and pay close attention to them, you'll always find examples of God working through others to care for people. This next activity is going to help us practice looking for God's goodness and grace in our world.

Instruct everyone to get back into their four groups from earlier. Give each group three or four newspapers and each participant a pair of scissors.

Say: **Take a few minutes to look through your group's newspapers and cut out all the articles you can find that illustrate ways God has provided for people.**

As the groups are cutting out articles, give each group two pieces of newsprint, markers, and a glue stick. After allowing groups time to cut out their articles, say: **Now we're going to put everything together and make a large newspaper that shows different ways God provides for people. Begin by folding both pieces of your group's newsprint in half like a newspaper. Next, take a few minutes to glue your personal journaling articles onto the newsprint, front and back. Also glue the newspaper articles you've cut out onto the newsprint. Finally, use markers to write your group's headlines from Ruth on your pieces of newsprint.** Allow about ten minutes for this activity.

WORSHIP TIME

When groups have finished their projects, have everyone find a partner. Say: **Boaz was Naomi and Ruth's kinsman-redeemer. If he hadn't agreed to take responsibility and care for them, they probably would have spent the rest of their lives in extreme poverty and hardship.**

Spend a moment reflecting on your life. Think of someone God provided in your life to be there for you in a time of need. It might be a parent, a friend, a teacher, a coach, a youth pastor, or someone else. When you've thought of someone, share with your

---

BONUS IDEAS

If time allows, have groups design artistic newspaper covers on the front of their newsprint, or have one of the groups—or an artistic person—design a cover for everyone.

partner your answers to these questions:
- Who was the person God provided in your life?
- In what way was this person there for you?
- What's one way that person was like Boaz?

Allow approximately five minutes for quiet discussion and sharing. Then have everyone form a prayer circle. Have participants take turns sharing the names of the people they identified. Afterward, pray or have a volunteer pray for the group. Be sure to give thanks for all the people God brings into our lives to be there for us just as Boaz was there for Ruth.

CLOSING

Instruct the teenagers to gather up all the pieces of newsprint their groups have created and assemble them into a single newspaper.

Say: **People have a tendency to dwell on the negative things that happen around them. As you probably noticed when cutting out articles in the newspapers, most of them are negative and report on bad news.** Ask:
- **What are some of the reasons people might fail to see God working in their lives?**

Say: **It's up to us as Christians to help others focus on the ways God provides for people. There are many ways we can do that. But we can begin by posting our newspaper in a conspicuous place in the church where others might see it and recognize that God does provide for us.**

Let the students decide where they'd like to put the newspaper to announce God's provision to others. If they need ideas, have them consider displaying the group newspaper in the youth room, in the worship area, on a bulletin board, or next to a church entrance. When they've decided on a location, have them put up the display for others to see.

Ask everyone to gather around the newspaper, and close the session with prayer. Ask that God use the efforts of the group to share God's message of love and care with others.

BONUS IDEAS

Consider hanging a bulletin board in the youth room or another prominent location in the church, where teenagers can post on an ongoing basis articles they find about God providing for people.

Feelings of a Stranger

Think of a time when you've felt like a stranger because you didn't know anyone.
Then use your artistic skills to illustrate how you felt in each situation described below.
Fill in the face with features that describe how you were feeling.

✸ How did you *feel* the night before the situation?

✸ What did you *feel* like when you arrived?

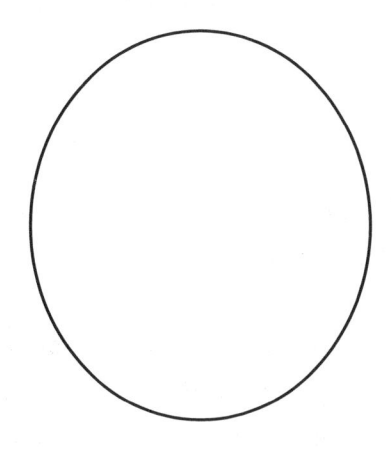

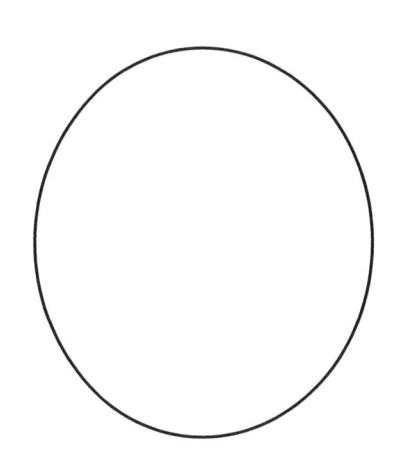

✸ How were you *feeling* when the event was about half over?

✸ How were you *feeling* when it was time to leave?

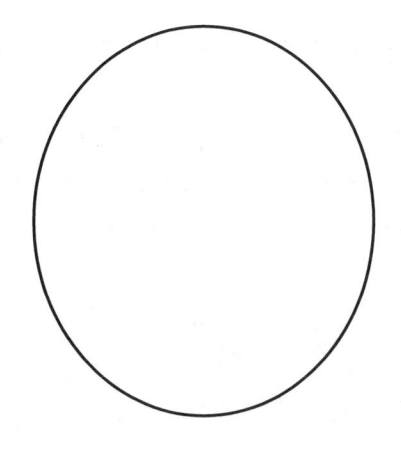

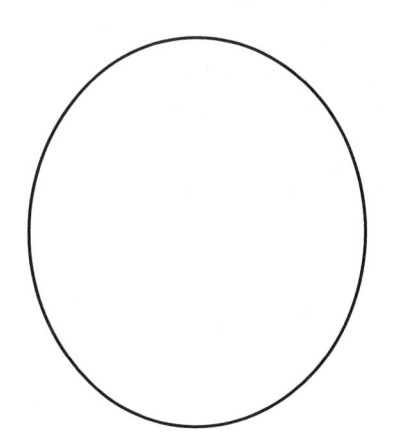

31

Permission to photocopy this handout from *Living Beyond Belief* granted for local church use. Copyright © Group Publishing, Inc., P.O. Box 481, Loveland, CO 80539.

Go to Shiloh

BIBLE CHARACTER: HANNAH

SCRIPTURE: 1 Samuel 1:1-20

THEME:
God hears our prayers.

SUPPLIES:
You'll need photocopies of the "ACE Listening Skills" handout (p. 37), a plastic foam cup, approximately two to three tablespoons of flour, a glass of water, a dry-erase board or newsprint and tape, a marker, Bibles, paper, and pens or pencils.

PREPARATION

Before the session, make one photocopy of the "ACE Listening Skills" handout (p. 37) for each person. Test the "missing water trick" from the Closing activity so you understand how the trick works. You may need to vary the amount of flour you use to make sure it will soak up all the water. After you understand how the trick works, put the appropriate amount of flour in a plastic foam cup and fill a glass with water.

Study 1 Samuel 1:1-20. Then read the entire session outline. Make sure all the activities fit your group, and make any necessary changes.

OVERVIEW

This study teaches students about Hannah's experience with God. It shows students how Hannah was faithful to pray regardless of her circumstances. Students will see that God can bring us joy even in the midst of trials. Students will

• realize that God wants them to be consistent in their prayer lives,

BIBLE BACKGROUND

You may want to share this background information with the students to help them gain insight into the story of Hannah.

Every year the Israelite males were required to go to the central sanctuary. In this area, the sanctuary was at Shiloh. At Shiloh they sacrificed animals as a way to celebrate God's provision in their lives. Shiloh was where the Israelites worshipped God and where Hannah went to pray.

Elkanah had gone against God's will when he took two wives. God's plan is for one man and one woman to be united only to each other (Matthew 19:5-8). However, righteous men throughout history have disobeyed God's marital design due to the lusts of their heart or because the wives they married were unable to produce children. This was the case for Elkanah and Hannah. Elkanah's success lay in his ability to continue his name. Therefore he married Peninnah in order to have an heir. Although it's clear in verse 5 that Elkanah preferred Hannah over Peninnah, Hannah still was distraught that she couldn't be a productive member in that society or fulfill her personal dream of having children.

• learn about the struggles and prayer life of Hannah,
• talk about one area of struggle in each of their lives and experience how God listens to them,
• worship God through prayer, and
• be reminded that God is always listening to them.

OPENER

Tape a piece of newsprint to the wall, or set up a dry-erase board where everyone can see it. Ask students to call out events that happen consistently regardless of circumstances. For example, the sun always rises, and people always get wet in the shower.

When you've compiled a list, ask:
• **Why is it important to have consistency in our lives?**
• **What would life be like if nothing was ever the same?**
• **What is one area of your life that feels consistent?**
• **What is one area of your life that doesn't feel consistent? How does that area of inconsistency affect you?**

UNDERSTANDING GOD'S WORD

Say: **God wants us to be consistent in our prayer lives. Our relationship with God shouldn't be dependent on what God is doing for us or how close we feel to God. Even though it may be hard for us to believe, God is listening to our prayers and will answer them at the right time. We need to trust that God hears us, and refuse to give up when God doesn't respond the way we'd like. It's important to worship God regardless of whether we feel like our prayers are answered.**

Ask several volunteers to read 1 Samuel 1:1-20 aloud, a verse at a time.

Have students form groups of four and answer the following questions:
• **Explain in your own words why Peninnah and Hannah weren't getting along.**

BIBLE BACKGROUND

You may want to share this background information with the students to help them gain insight into the story of Hannah.

It's significant that even though Hannah struggled with being childless and Elkanah struggled as he watched her suffer, they both continued to worship God year after year. As faithfully as Peninnah taunted Hannah, Hannah served the Lord.

When Hannah cried out that she wanted God to remember her, she wasn't saying she believed God had forgotten her. She wanted God to take action in answering her prayers. After Hannah received a blessing from the priest, she still worshipped God. Her love for God was consistent regardless of what God did.

Hannah made a vow to the Lord as a way of acknowledging her dependence on God. Hannah knew it was God who could open her womb and give her a child. By making her vow, Hannah was saying that the child would belong to God. She obligated her son to take a Nazirite vow (Judges 13:7). "Nazirite" means "to separate or consecrate" to God. By committing her child to a Nazirite vow, she was

continued on page 35

• Both Peninnah and Hannah were discontent. How did the two women deal with their unhappiness?

• What do you think Hannah learned from this life trial?

• Why do you think Hannah felt so much better after her time of prayer?

• What can we learn from Hannah's prayer?

• Why do you think God wants us to be consistent in our prayer life?

APPLYING GOD'S WORD

Say: Hannah prayed for many years before God answered her prayer and gave her a son. During this time of waiting, she probably wondered if God was listening to her cry out. Sometimes it's hard to pray because we feel like we're talking to a blank wall or we don't even know how to approach God.

Take students outside and have them look up at the moon. If you're meeting during the day and the moon isn't visible, point out where the moon will be visible in several hours. Point out that the way we experience the moon is very similar to the way we can experience God.

Ask:

• If you can see the moon, what shape does it appear to be?

• What is the actual shape of the moon? How do you know?

• Is there anything hindering you from seeing the moon? If so, what?

• If you can't see the moon, how do you know it's there?

Say: Even when the moon appears to be gone, we know by experience and knowledge that it's still there and it always will be there. Even when it appears to change shape, we know it's always round. The fact that the moon exists isn't based on what we can see. In the same way, I encourage you to believe God is listening to your prayers even when you can't sense God.

Bring students back to your meeting area, and give each person a photocopy of the "ACE Listening Skills" handout. Give students a few minutes to read through the handout, and clarify any questions they have. Help students understand the difference between

> *continued from page 34*
>
> vowing to have her child be separate from the world and devoted to God.
>
> Although Hannah prayed without sound, she trusted that God knew her heart's desire. When she entered the tabernacle she felt distressed and hopeless. She left her time with God feeling peaceful and full of hope. God answered her deeper prayer for contentment before even providing for her specific need. When she trusted God, she felt a deep sense of contentment.

hearing someone and really listening.

Say: **Find a partner and talk with that person about a struggle in your life. Your partner also will share with you. As you're listening to your partner share, use the listening skills on the handout I've given you.**

Give the first partner in each pair about five minutes to talk, then give the other partner about a minute to respond. Then have the other partner share for five minutes and the first partner respond. When pairs are finished sharing, ask partners to pray short prayers for each other, either aloud or silently.

When pairs are finished praying, say: **We all face struggles in life, and we will for as long as we live. It can be hard to know how to handle our struggles. Maybe you've never talked to God, or maybe you have a hard time believing God hears you and cares about you. It's true: God wants you to take your deepest troubles to him. And God will listen to you even better than your partner did. You'll have God's full attention.**

WORSHIP TIME

Say: **As Christians, it's important to learn how to worship God in our private prayer lives. We have a tendency to think worship happens only when we're singing, but we can worship any time, anywhere, doing anything as long as our hearts are focused on God in adoration.**

Give each person a pen or pencil and a piece of paper. Ask students to find a place by themselves and read 1 Samuel 2:1-10. Then instruct them to paraphrase or rewrite Hannah's prayer in their own words. Encourage students to focus on making Hannah's prayer their own prayer.

When students are finished writing, gather everyone back together and allow volunteers to read their prayers aloud.

CLOSING

Hold up the plastic foam cup with flour in the bottom. When you have everyone's attention, pour about two tablespoons of water from the glass into the plastic foam cup. As you pour the water, turn the cup around so students can see that the water did go into the cup. This also will stall for time as the water soaks into the flour. Next hold the cup upside down. The water should have absorbed into the flour and shouldn't pour out.

Say: **The water is still in the cup even though you can't see it. And God is here even though we can't see him.**

Show students the flour in the bottom of the cup. Say: **Prayer is a mystery. We can understand it only partially until we go to heaven. In the meantime, we can trust that God hears our prayers.**

ACE Listening Skills

Put these listening skills into practice as you listen to your partner.

Attention

Create a "bubble of attention" around the person you're listening to. This means you listen with your body language and eye contact. Listen to the other person as if you're watching the most interesting movie you've ever seen.

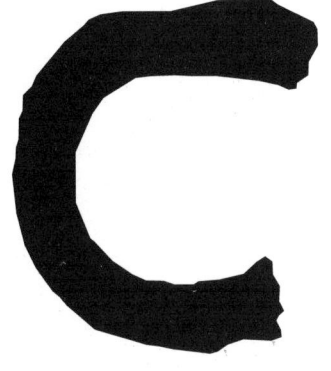

Clarify

After your partner is finished sharing, ask several questions to make sure you understood correctly. For example, you may want to ask something like "When you said you were frustrated, what made you frustrated?" or "Are you trying to say that you wish your sister would leave you alone while you're with your friends?"

Empathize

Show your partner that you understand how he or she feels. You could say something like "That sounds really hard" or "I get in fights with my mom, too."

Nothing Separates Us

DAVID

BIBLE CHARACTER:

SCRIPTURE: 2 Samuel 11:1-17, 26–12:17; Psalms 32; 51; 103; Romans 8:38-39

THEME:
God loves us unconditionally.

SUPPLIES:
You'll need photocopies of the "Observing Love" handout (p. 44), a book, paper, newsprint, tape, marker, and Bibles.

PREPARATION

Before the session, make six photocopies of the "Observing Love" handout (p. 44).

Study the Scripture passages listed above. Then read the entire session outline. Make sure all the activities fit your group, and make any necessary changes.

OVERVIEW

This session teaches students about David's experience with God. It reminds students that God loves us unconditionally, even when we turn away from God in sin. Students will
- define unconditional love;
- compare their response, David's own response, and God's response to David's sin;
- explore how they've experienced God's love in their own lives;
- find scriptural assurance of God's unconditional love; and

38

• sing love songs to celebrate God's unconditional love.

OPENER

Ask six students to perform a skit for the rest of the group. If you'd like fewer than six students to perform the skit, have two teenagers play the roles of all the "videotaped" examples of love. You'll need the following roles: Scientist, Parent, Child, Pupil, Teacher, and Praying Person.

The Pupil will need a book and a piece of paper. Give each performer a photocopy of the "Observing Love" handout (p. 44), and ask performers to rehearse quietly in one area of the room.

As the performers rehearse the skit, ask everyone else to form pairs and create a definition of the phrase "unconditional love." As pairs discuss, tape a sheet of newsprint to a wall, and draw a horizontal line in the middle of the newsprint. After a few minutes of discussion, ask each pair to share its definition. Write the definitions on the top half of the sheet of newsprint. Then ask the group to decide upon one definition, and write that definition in large letters on the bottom half of the sheet of newsprint.

Call all the students together, and ask the performers to perform the skit for the rest of the students. Ask the audience members to evaluate, as they watch, whether the examples they see in the skit meet the definition of unconditional love they created.

After the skit, lead teenagers in applauding the performers. Then ask:

• **How were the segments of "videotape" in the skit similar?**

• **What, if anything, did the skit demonstrate about unconditional love? What, if anything, was the skit missing?**

• **Does being loved unconditionally mean you can do anything you want with no consequences? Explain.**

• **Do you think God loves us unconditionally? Why or why not?**

Say: **Let's turn to the Bible to help us answer those last two questions. We'll evaluate what an incident in the life of King David of Israel tells us about God's love for us.**

BIBLE BACKGROUND

You may want to share this background information with your students to help them understand the story of David.

When David summoned Bathsheba to his palace, he was following the behavior of other despotic kings of the East; when they wanted a woman, they simply sent their officers to her house to bring her to the palace. But as Israelites, David and Bathsheba had more at stake with the public than other kings did. Their very lives were at stake, for the law as written in Leviticus 20:10 stated that adulterers and adulteresses should be put to death. David, who was not just a political leader but also a religious leader, sacrificed his character. Because of his behavior, he lost the high respect of his own family and his public.

UNDERSTANDING GOD'S WORD

If you have more than ten students, you may want to have them form two groups for this activity, with each group following the same instructions. Explain that students are going to play the role of a jury who must decide how to sentence the defendant in the case of the State vs. King David of Israel. Have the jury sit together and prepare to hear "witnesses."

Begin by reviewing the story of David. Say: **David was a shepherd, the youngest son in his family, and was chosen by God to be the king of Israel. David served King Saul of Israel as a musician and soldier, and his success in battle made him popular with the public. Saul became jealous and tried to kill David, but David always escaped. When Saul died in battle, the people named David king of Israel.**

Now as you listen to these witnesses, you must track the king's behavior and determine an appropriate sentence.

Call a volunteer to stand in front of the jury as the first witness, and ask the witness to read aloud 2 Samuel 11:1-4. Ask:

• **What's your response to King David's behavior?**

Ask a second witness to stand in front of the jury and read aloud 2 Samuel 11:5-13. Ask:

• **What do you think King David is hoping to accomplish here?**

• **Do you think this is the appropriate action for King David to take? Why or why not?**

Have another witness stand in front of the jury and read aloud 2 Samuel 11:14-17. Ask the jury to discuss the following question and determine an appropriate sentence:

• **Now what's your response to King David's behavior, especially considering that he was not only a political leader, but also a religious leader?**

After a couple of minutes of discussion, ask the jury to name their sentence. If they haven't decided upon a sentence, ask them to name the options they're considering. Then say: **Let's see what happened next. Listen for the sentence King David pronounced upon himself.** Ask a volunteer to read aloud 2 Samuel 11:26–12:6. Ask:

40

• What sentence did David unknowingly pronounce upon himself?

• What's your reaction to that sentence?

Say: **Now let's see what God's reaction was to King David's behavior.** Ask a volunteer to read aloud 2 Samuel 12:7-17. Ask:

• **Do you think this was a fair sentence? Explain.**

• **Do you think David thought this was a fair sentence? Explain.**

• **What do you think it meant to David that the Lord took away his sin?**

• **Does unconditional love mean we don't face natural consequences of our sin or that we aren't disciplined when we sin? Explain.**

• **What message do you think it would have sent to Israel if God had not responded to David's sin?**

• **Do you think God's response fits the definition of unconditional love you created earlier? Why or why not?**

Say: **Now I'd like you to examine David's response to God's sentence by reading psalms he wrote.** Have students form three groups, and ask each group to read one of the following psalms: Psalms 32; 51; and 103. After groups have read, ask them to summarize the message for the rest of the groups. Ask:

• **How did David feel about his sin? about God's response to his sin?**

• **Do you think David felt loved unconditionally by God? Explain.**

• **How did God's love affect David's life?**

Have students summarize what they've learned about God's unconditional love through David's experiences.

APPLYING GOD'S WORD

Have students remain in their groups to discuss the following questions:

• **During what experiences have you felt God's love?**

• **When have you experienced God's forgiveness?**

• **Have you faced sin's consequences or God's discipline? Explain.**

• What difference has God's love made in your life?

• What's your reaction to God for loving us unconditionally?

• How can God's unconditional love change the way you look at life?

• How can God's love affect your behavior when you sin or when you need help or support?

Tell groups you'd like them to create a two-minute talk show titled "God's Unconditional Love in Our Lives." Explain that the talk show should focus on how God's love affects people's lives. Ask groups to incorporate the definition of unconditional love they created at the beginning of the session. Emphasize that groups should create the talk shows based on group members' own experiences. For example, a group could plan to have one member act as the talk-show host and the other members act as guests. The host could introduce the show with the definition of unconditional love the class created and could then ask each guest to tell about times they've experienced God's unconditional love.

As groups prepare, circulate to offer any direction or help needed. After about ten minutes, have groups take turns acting out their talk shows for the class. Be sure to applaud each group's presentation.

WORSHIP TIME

Have teenagers open their Bibles to Romans 8:38-39. Explain that students are going to participate in a prayerful responsive reading in which you'll ask a question and they'll answer by reading aloud Romans 8:38-39. Read aloud the following:

Say: **Lord, the Bible says you *are* love, but we don't always feel very loved. Can we trust that you love us even when we don't feel it?**

Have students respond by reading Romans 8:38-39.

Say: **Lord, it seems like the world is becoming a scarier and scarier place. Does that mean you've gone away or taken your love from us?**

Have students respond by reading Romans 8:38-39.

Say: **Lord, what about our sin? We sin again and again—don't you stop loving us after we sin so many times?**

Have students respond by reading Romans 8:38-39.

Say: **Lord, when we sin and you don't remove the consequences or when you discipline us, does that mean you've stopped loving us?**

Have students respond by reading Romans 8:38-39.

Say: **Lord, it's wonderful to be reassured that nothing in all creation will take your love from us. Thank you so much for loving us unconditionally. In Jesus' name, amen.**

CLOSING

Have students form three groups. Ask each group to think of a love song that reflects what God's love means to them. Assure students that the song can be something simple such as "Jesus Loves Me" or can be a contemporary song about God's love. After students have prepared for a couple of minutes, have each group perform its love song. Applaud each group's performance. Afterward, close in prayer, thanking God for unconditional love.

Observing Love

Scientist: *(Standing in the middle of the "stage" and facing the audience.)* I'm pleased to offer to you at this time my study titled "The Affective Emotional Response From Homogenous Species of Natural Community and the Reciprocal Apportionment of Affective Behaviors." Momentarily you will have the opportunity to observe behaviors arising in various spontaneous conditions which I videotaped as models for the resulting study. Please observe the ensuing segment of videotape, in which I investigated a child and its parent.

(The Scientist moves to the side, and the Parent and Child begin walking slowly across the stage. The Child runs ahead of the parent and back.)

Parent: Jamie, please stop running. The ground is slippery from the rain, and you could fall down.

(Child walks a few steps with the Parent; then the Child runs ahead again, slips, falls, and cries loudly. The Parent runs to the Child, comforts the Child, and dries the tears.)

Parent: OK, Jamie, you're fine. *(Child stops crying but continues to sniffle.)* You've scraped your knee a bit, but you're OK. On we go.

(Parent and Child walk offstage.)

Scientist: Now please observe this exchange between a mathematical instructor and a pupil.

(Teacher stands at the middle of the stage, and Pupil walks in holding a book and a piece of paper.)

Pupil: I messed up again! Can you please help me get this math problem right?

(Pupil hands Teacher the paper.)

Teacher: Terry, tell me the formula for finding the circumference of a circle.

Pupil: Um…I can't remember.

Teacher: It's in your book, Terry.

Pupil: *(Fumbles through the book, stops, and reads.)* Oh yeah, it's two times pi times the radius.

Teacher: That's great, Terry! Now look at what you've done here…

(As Scientist speaks, Pupil and Teacher walk offstage. Praying Person walks to the middle of the stage and kneels, hands folded and head bowed.)

Scientist: Please indulge my inclination to share with you one final segment, an exceptionally interesting sample. Please observe.

Praying Person: I am blessed because you've forgiven me, Lord. When I tried to hide my sin from you, the truth of what I'd done never left me. I was in agony. But when I confessed my sin to you, you forgave me. Thank you for your love!

God Speaks

BIBLE CHARACTER: ELIJAH

SCRIPTURE: 1 Kings 19:1-16

THEME:
God speaks to us.

SUPPLIES:
You'll need photocopies of the "Elijah's Travels" handout (p. 51), pens or pencils, Bibles, and paper.

PREPARATION

Before the session, make one photocopy of the "Elijah's Travels" handout (p. 51) for each student.

Study 1 Kings 17:1–19:16. Then read the entire session outline. Make sure all the activities fit your group, and make any necessary changes.

OVERVIEW

This session teaches students about Elijah's experience with God. It reminds students that God speaks to us in many ways and that we must listen to hear God speaking. Students will

• wait for spoken direction,

• compare Elijah's experiences when he waited for God to speak and when he didn't wait for God to speak,

• discover various ways God has spoken to them and how it has affected their lives,

• think about how to discern God's "voice," and

• pray for God to direct them.

45

OPENER

Instruct students to walk around, greeting each other and shaking each other's hands until they receive further instructions. Emphasize that even if they see other people doing something different and even if they've talked to everyone already, they're to continue greeting each other and shaking each other's hands.

Have teenagers begin. After a minute or two, approach each student one by one and whisper in his or her ear: **Please stop greeting people, and go sit down in a circle now.** Direct the teenagers slowly, whispering to one person every ten or twenty seconds, until only one student remains. Be sure the one student who's left won't be shy or embarrassed about being the center of attention. Finally, after another ten to twenty seconds, whisper the same direction in the last student's ear.

When everyone is seated in the circle, ask:
- **What was it like to have to wait for directions?**
- **What was frustrating about this activity?**
- **How did you feel when you finally got your instructions?**
- **How was this exercise like waiting for God to speak to you?**

Say: **Sometimes we feel like we're just walking around in a circle, getting nowhere, and we need direction. We'd especially like for God to speak to us to let us know what we should do. Today we're going to explore the story of the prophet Elijah. Elijah was at the end of his rope, and he needed direction. Elijah listened for God, and God spoke to Elijah. God speaks to us, too.**

UNDERSTANDING GOD'S WORD

Give each person a photocopy of the "Elijah's Travels" handout (p. 51) and a pen or pencil, and ask teenagers to form two groups. Review the story of Elijah with students, using the map on the handout as a visual guide. Say: **Elijah was a prophet of God. He tried to convince the people that God is the one true God so they'd stop worshipping idols. Elijah proved God's singular power again and again. First Elijah warned King Ahab of a drought that would end**

BIBLE BACKGROUND

You may want to share this background information with your students to help them understand the story of Elijah.

Elijah was raised in Gilead—whose people generally followed Israel's strict traditions and worshipped only God—during a time when other gods were influencing Israel's culture. King Omri of Israel, whose lands included a large number of Canaanites, encouraged the worship of the Canaanite god Baal. To forge a political alliance with Canaanite Phoenicia, Omri arranged for his son Ahab to marry the Phoenician princess Jezebel. Jezebel fervently worshipped Baal and the goddess Asherah, and she worked to suppress the worship of God. As king, Ahab built a temple to Baal and apparently wanted Baal and God to be worshipped equally. This situation was simply unacceptable for those, such as Elijah, who worshipped only God.

only when Elijah said it would. During the drought, God told Elijah where to go to survive. After several years of drought, God told Elijah to visit King Ahab again. When Elijah did, he challenged the prophets of the god Baal to a contest on Mount Carmel. After the prophets of Baal failed miserably, Elijah prepared a water-soaked altar and offering; then he asked God to cause a fire to burn the offering. God responded immediately with a fire that burned up the offering, wood, stones, soil, and water. Then, finally, the people believed that God alone was the one true God. After this success, Elijah ran all the way back to town.

Explain that groups will use the map on the handout to record what happened to Elijah next. Ask one group's members to read 1 Kings 19:1-16 and note on their maps where Elijah went, then mark the places where the Bible specifically states that God spoke to Elijah, and write down what Elijah did as a result. Ask the other group's members to read 1 Kings 19:1-16 and note on their maps where Elijah went, mark the places where the Bible doesn't specifically state that God spoke to Elijah, and write down Elijah's actions during those times.

Give groups about ten minutes to complete their maps, and then get their attention again. Have everyone discuss the following questions as one big group. Encourage students to use their maps as visual guides as they answer the questions. Ask:

• **When did God speak to Elijah, and what did Elijah do as a result?**

• **What different ways did God speak to Elijah?**

• **Why do you think God spoke to Elijah in different ways?**

• **When did Elijah act without God's spoken direction, and what happened as a result?**

• **Why do you think God chose not to speak to Elijah sometimes?**

• **Compare what happened to Elijah when he waited for God to speak and when he acted without waiting for God to speak.**

Ask a volunteer to read aloud 1 Kings 19:9-13, and then ask:

• **How do you think Elijah felt before God spoke to him?**
• **How did Elijah listen for God to speak?**

BIBLE BACKGROUND

You may want to share this background information with your students to help them understand the story of Elijah.

After Baal's defeat on Mount Carmel, the Israelites killed Baal's prophets. Because of the pervading mood, Queen Jezebel probably wouldn't have dared to carry out her death threat against Elijah. "Had he remained steadfast and immovable, the impression on the mind of Ahab and the people generally might have been followed by good results" (*Jamieson, Fausset and Brown's Commentary,* www.biblestudytools.net). But Elijah didn't remain steadfast, so the queen's threats worked. Without waiting for God to speak, Elijah abandoned his post and ran for his life.

• What do you think the wind, earthquake, and fire signify? the whisper?

• How did God's words on the mountain affect Elijah?

• What do Elijah's experiences tell you about how God speaks to us?

Say: After the victory on Mount Carmel, Elijah probably was elated. When his life was threatened, Elijah's elation turned to fear and desperation. God hadn't abandoned Elijah, though. On the contrary, God sent an angel to care for Elijah, reaffirmed his power, and then gently directed Elijah about what he should do next. God spoke to Elijah, and Elijah listened.

APPLYING GOD'S WORD

Say: **Just as God spoke to Elijah, God speaks to us**—and in many different ways. Maybe you feel assurance from God when you see a sunrise, or maybe you read the Bible to receive direction from God.

Distribute paper and pens or pencils, and explain that teenagers will have five minutes to circulate and interview each other about different ways God has spoken to them. Ask each person to interview at least three other people. Suggest that teenagers ask each other questions such as "When has God spoken to you?" "What different ways has God spoken to you?" and "What happened as a result?"

When everyone understands the task, have students begin circulating and interviewing each other. After about five minutes, call everyone back together again. Have teenagers form groups of three with people they didn't interview. Have trio members share what they discovered about the different ways God has spoken to people and the effects God's speaking had on their lives. Then have trios discuss how God has spoken to them or could have been speaking to them in the same ways. Then have trios discuss the following questions:

• What difference does God make in our lives when he speaks to us?

• What difference does it make when you listen for God to speak?

• **How might you remember to listen for God to speak?**

Based on what they've learned, ask each trio to create a one-sentence reminder to listen for God to speak. For example, a group may say, "Listening for God is active, not passive." Then ask each trio to state its sentence.

WORSHIP TIME

Ask:

• **How did Elijah know when God was speaking to him?**
• **How do *you* know when God is the one speaking?**

Be sure students have paper and pens. Say: **If we're going to listen to God, we need to learn to discern when God is the one speaking.** Explain that you'll read verses from God's Word and that students should respond by completing the following sentence for each verse: "God, I'll know you're the one speaking to me because you…" When everyone understands, have students get by themselves. Then read aloud the following verses from the Bible, allowing time after each verse for students to write:

• "God is our refuge and strength, an ever-present help in trouble" (Psalm 46:1).
• "Be still, and know that I am God; I will be exalted among the nations, I will be exalted in the earth" (Psalm 46:10).
• "For the Lord gives wisdom, and from his mouth come knowledge and understanding" (Proverbs 2:6).
• "If a kingdom is divided against itself, that kingdom cannot stand" (Mark 3:24).
• "It is impossible for God to lie" (Hebrews 6:18b).
• "When tempted, no one should say, 'God is tempting me.' For God cannot be tempted by evil, nor does he tempt anyone" (James 1:13).
• "God is love" (1 John 4:16b).
• "Perfect love drives out fear" (1 John 4:18b).

CLOSING

Say: **God will speak to us in many different ways just as he spoke to Elijah. Let's pray now and ask God to speak to us about situations in our own lives. And remember that in order to hear God speak, we have to listen.** Explain that you'll begin the prayer and that students will silently complete the sentences you begin. Also explain that you'll leave time for quiet listening after each sentence.

Pray: **Dear God, we sometimes are so excited and enthusiastic about our victories. We want to thank you now for these exciting situations in our lives.** Pause.

Like Elijah, we sometimes become afraid. We'd like to ask you to guide us through these situations that we're fearful about. Pause.

Like Elijah, we sometimes take action without listening for you to speak. We need your guidance to lead us back to the right path. Please redirect our steps in these situations. Pause.

Like Elijah, we're trying to learn to listen to you, God. Thank you for meeting us, speaking to us, and gently guiding us. Amen.

You may want to allow some time for teenagers to share what they feel God is saying to them.

Elijah's Travels

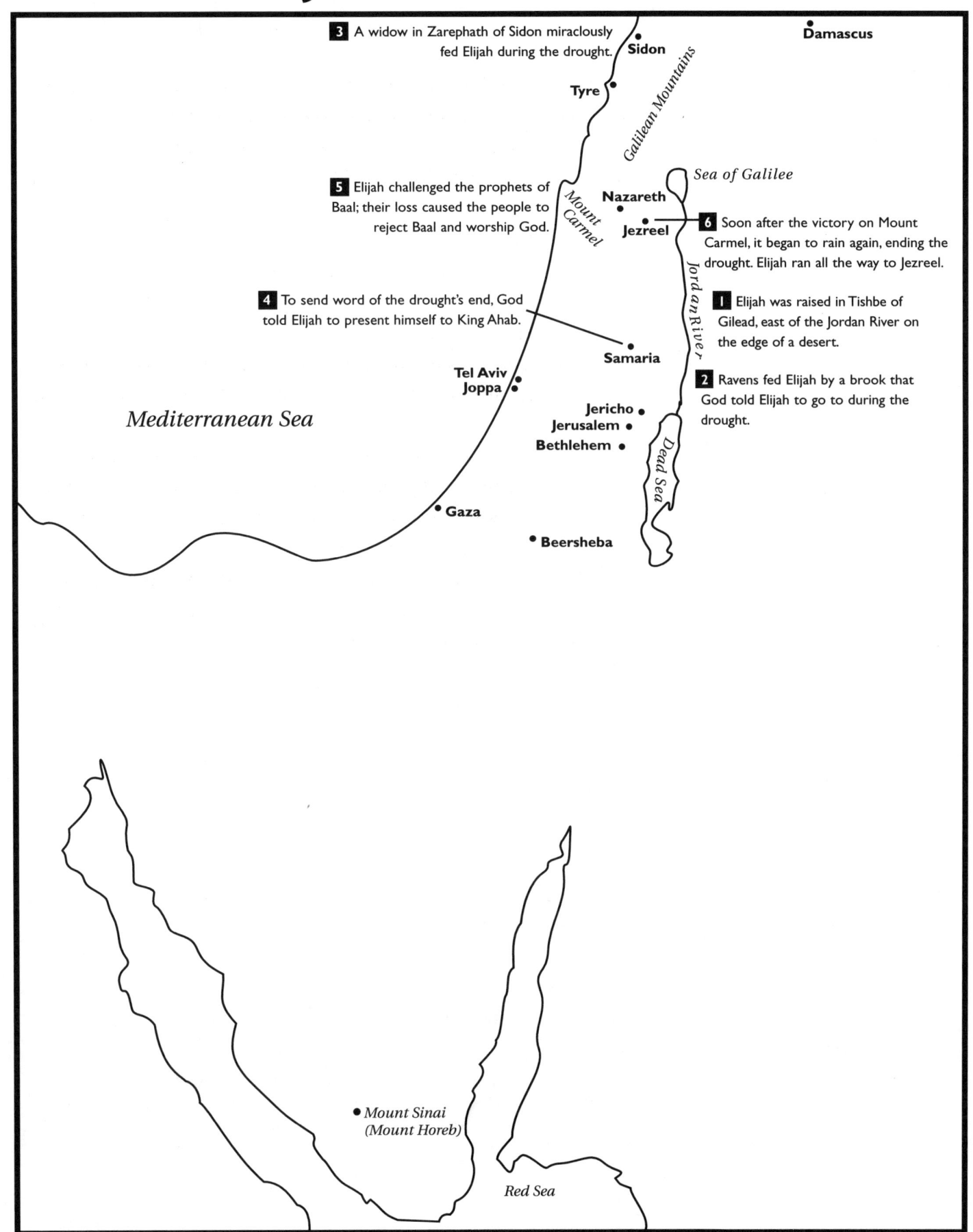

3 A widow in Zarephath of Sidon miraculously fed Elijah during the drought.

● Sidon
● Damascus
● Tyre
Galilean Mountains

Sea of Galilee
Nazareth

5 Elijah challenged the prophets of Baal; their loss caused the people to reject Baal and worship God.

Mount Carmel
Jezreel

6 Soon after the victory on Mount Carmel, it began to rain again, ending the drought. Elijah ran all the way to Jezreel.

Jordan River

1 Elijah was raised in Tishbe of Gilead, east of the Jordan River on the edge of a desert.

4 To send word of the drought's end, God told Elijah to present himself to King Ahab.

● Samaria

2 Ravens fed Elijah by a brook that God told Elijah to go to during the drought.

Tel Aviv
Joppa

Mediterranean Sea

● Jericho
● Jerusalem
● Bethlehem

Dead Sea

● Gaza
● Beersheba

● *Mount Sinai (Mount Horeb)*

Red Sea

Permission to photocopy this handout from *Living Beyond Belief* granted for local church use. Copyright © Group Publishing, Inc., P.O. Box 481, Loveland, CO 80539.

An Unlikely Hero

BIBLE CHARACTER:

SCRIPTURE:

Esther 4:1–5:8; 7:1-6

THEME:
God calls us.

SUPPLIES:
You'll need photocopies of the "Hero Profiles" handout (p. 58), paper, pens or pencils, Bibles, newsprint, markers, and tape.

PREPARATION

Before the session, make one photocopy of the "Hero Profiles" handout (p. 58) for each person.

Study Esther 4:1–5:8; 7:1-6. Then read the entire session outline. Make sure all the activities fit your group, and make any necessary changes.

OVERVIEW

This session teaches students about Esther's experience with God. It reminds students that God calls us to act. Students will
- discuss traits of real-life heroes,
- learn how Esther became a real-life hero,
- describe events in their own lives in which God may be or may have been calling them,
- thank God for calling people, and
- demonstrate that they're ready to respond to God's call.

OPENER

Have teenagers form groups of four, and then have groups discuss what makes a person a real-life hero. Emphasize that instead of talking about fictional superheroes, you'd like the groups to talk about real-life heroes.

After a few minutes of discussion, explain that each group should use what they've discussed to create a real-life hero and prepare to present its hero. Tell groups that everyone should participate in the presentation, with one person acting out the role of the real-life hero and the other group members describing the hero in a creative way, such as with a "scientific" description, song or rap, poem, or story. For example, one group member might pretend to be a doctor who helps children in Third World countries. The rest of the group can describe that person by telling a story of someone the doctor has helped.

Give groups about five minutes to work, and then ask each group to present its hero. Afterward, ask:

• **Have you known any real-life heroes? Explain.**

• **Do you think God sometimes calls people to be heroes? Explain.**

• **Do you think you could be a real-life hero by responding to God's call? Explain.**

Say: **The word "hero" often conjures up movie-screen images of steely-eyed, muscle-bound people who jump from moving trains or cling onto the hoods of speeding cars. Truthfully, though, heroes usually are just normal, everyday people who are all around us. Perhaps even we are heroes. We may not know we're heroes until God calls us to act. Today you'll learn about one unlikely hero God called.**

UNDERSTANDING GOD'S WORD

Have teenagers stay in their groups of four, and distribute paper and pens or pencils. Review the story of Esther with your students, reminding them that Esther was an orphaned Jewish girl who had been exiled from Jerusalem with other Jews, including her older cousin Mordecai, who had cared for her as his daughter. Also remind students that Esther had been chosen to be part of the king's harem, had kept her Jewish heritage a secret, and had eventually become King Xerxes' queen. Finally remind students that while Esther was queen, King Xerxes had agreed to allow all the Jews to be killed.

Have the groups read Esther 4:1–5:8; 7:1-6 and note as they read how God called Esther. After groups have read the Scripture, ask:

• **What did Esther receive from others that led her to approach the king?**

• **What role did Mordecai play in this event?**

• **How did Mordecai view Esther's rise to the position of queen?** (See Esther 4:14.)

Have each group write a newspaper article explaining how Esther was an unlikely hero called by God. Encourage groups to think about what they learned from their discussions and the Scripture to help them explain how Esther was called by God. After groups have written their articles, have them read their articles aloud. Then ask:

• **How does Esther's story show that God called her?**

• **How did Esther become aware of God's calling in her life?**

• **What does it teach you, if anything, that God never spoke directly to Esther or Mordecai in the entire book of Esther—that, in fact, God's name is never mentioned?**

Say: **Esther was nobody, an orphaned Jewish girl far from home. Then suddenly she became queen just before her people desperately needed an advocate. Without Esther's action, the Jews would have been annihilated. Esther didn't perform miracles; and as far as we know, she didn't even hear God's voice or have visions or dreams. But through the information and encouragement of others, she realized that God was calling her to act.**

BIBLE BACKGROUND

You may want to share this background information with your students to help them understand the story of Esther.

King Xerxes was described by the Greek historian Herodotus as a "cruel, capricious, sensual man" (David Alexander, ed., et. al., *Eerdmans' Handbook to the Bible*). The book of Esther confirms this, as the king deposed his queen because she wouldn't make an exhibition of herself at one of the king's parties; later the king agreed to allow all the Jews to be killed.

In chapter 4, Esther cites a law which stated that a person could not approach the king without being summoned. The law forced all business and petitions to be transacted via the king's ministers. If a person broke the law, he or she could be put to death unless the king excused the breach. Knowing King Xerxes' personality and the strictness of Persian law, Esther had sufficient reason to be afraid.

APPLYING GOD'S WORD

Have teenagers form pairs and discuss these questions:

• **Can you think of other people throughout history or in your own life who God called to act? Explain.**

• **How did those people know that God was calling them?**

• **In what different ways does God call us?**

• **What kinds of things do you think God calls people to do?**

Distribute the "Hero Profiles" handouts (p. 58), and ask pairs to read them together. After each profile, ask pairs to think of situations in their own lives in which God could be calling or did call them to act in the same way—to help a friend, to teach someone about Jesus, or to stand up for what's right, for example. You may want to tell teenagers about a situation from your own life to give them some direction. Have pairs tell each other about those situations and discuss how they could react when God calls them to be real-life heroes.

Distribute newsprint and markers. Then ask pairs to help each other draw comic strips featuring themselves as real-life heroes responding to God's call in their own lives. For example, Zoe could draw herself teaching a neighbor's child to read after school, or Justin could draw himself standing up to his teammates' pressure to take steroids.

When students have finished drawing, ask everyone to present his or her comic strip. Afterward, ask:

• **What does it take to be a real-life hero?**

• **How can you listen for God's call in your life?**

• **How can people around you help you respond to God's call?**

• **What difference does God make in our lives when he calls us?**

• **What difference does God make in other people's lives when he calls us?**

WORSHIP TIME

Say: **When we respond to God's call as Esther did, we may affect ourselves, a few other people, or entire nations. People such as Harriet Tubman, a Civil War–era slave who led other** slaves to freedom; Mother Teresa, a nun who founded charities that care for destitute people; and Martin Luther, the reformer who translated the Bible into the German language, have made a difference in the world by responding to God's call.

Ask students to form a circle. Place a sheet of newsprint and markers in the middle of the circle. Label the newsprint "God Calls Heroes." Then ask students to think of all the people they can who have responded to God's call—people both historical and current, people they've read about or know personally. Give students a few minutes to write the names of those heroes on the sheet of newsprint.

After students are finished writing names, ask teenagers to explain why they wrote down the names they did and how God made a difference in the world by calling those people. For example, Cherie may explain that she wrote the name Clara Barton because Clara Barton founded the American Red Cross, an organization that makes a difference by helping people in need.

When everyone has shared, tell the group they're going to thank God for using people to make such a difference in the world. Ask students to go around the circle, say the name of one of the heroes, and thank God for the difference he has made by calling that hero to act.

Start the prayer of thanksgiving yourself, and then ask volunteers to pray about at least one hero. When everyone who wants to has prayed, close the prayer by saying something like this: **You call ordinary people to do your work, and you change the world every time. Thank you for giving us the opportunity to be heroes for you, and thank you for changing our world by calling ordinary people to be heroes. Amen.**

CLOSING

Have students remain in the circle, and ask:

• How does it feel to know that God calls you?

Say: **God may call us in many ways to do many different things. Each time, God makes a difference in our lives and in our world.**

The heroes we normally think about are fictional superheroes such as Superman. He has a large S on his shirt and is known for being faster than a speeding bullet. But today you've learned that ordinary people like you and me are real-life heroes when we respond to God's call.

Ask students to think of symbols or slogans for themselves to represent that they're ready to be heroes by responding to God's call. Have teenagers draw their symbols or write their slogans on the "God Calls Heroes" sheet of newsprint. Then tape the sheet of newsprint to a wall as a reminder for students to respond to God's call.

Hero Profiles

Coincidental Man

Victor usually took the city bus home, but he felt like walking today. Because he chose to walk, he just happened to see one of his good friends picking a fight with another guy over a misunderstanding. Victor knew his friend would be mad if he got in the way, and the fight wasn't any of his business anyway. But Victor also knew he was in the right place at the right time, and he decided to act before his friend hurt someone.

Gifted Girl

Tara's best subject was math, and she always got great grades. From simple addition to complicated calculus theories, the language of math just made sense to her. Tara's mom mentioned that their neighbor's son was having trouble in math class, and Tara knew she could help. It meant less personal time on some weekday evenings, but Tara decided to act so the boy could understand math.

Encouraged Elisa

Everyone always said Elisa was great with kids. One day Elisa's friend Tony told her about a camp for troubled kids that was looking for counselors. Elisa wasn't sure she would be able to work with troubled kids, but Tony assured her she'd do great. When Elisa talked to her family and friends about the camp, they all encouraged her to apply. Elisa knew she was good with kids, and she trusted her friends and family to lead her in the right direction. Elisa decided to act.

Reflective Ron

Ron had been curious about mission work for a long time. He went on every mission trip his church offered, and he thought a lot about working full time with a missions organization. It was a tough decision, though, because Ron knew he'd be far away from his family and in difficult conditions. To help him decide if God was calling him, Ron prayed and studied the Bible. After several months of reflection, Ron decided to act.

The Power of Protection

BIBLE CHARACTER: DANIEL

SCRIPTURE: Daniel 6:1-28

THEME:
God protects us.

SUPPLIES:
You'll need photocopies of "The Power of Protection" handout (p. 64) and "The Worship of Protection" handout (p. 65), masking tape, four 4x4-foot sheets of cardboard, scissors, markers, a large supply of scrap paper, Bibles, pens or pencils, index cards, and one large cross or a drawing of a cross on a sheet of newsprint.

PREPARATION

Before the session, make three photocopies of "The Power of Protection" handout (p. 64) and four photocopies of "The Worship of Protection" handout (p. 65). Use masking tape to divide your meeting area into four separate territories.

Study Daniel 6:1-28. Then read the entire session outline. Make sure all the activities fit your group, and make any necessary changes.

OVERVIEW

This session teaches students about Daniel's experience with God. It reminds students that God's protection is reliable and unending. Even though they might feel like God has forgotten them, they'll be reminded that they can trust God to protect them. Students will

• talk about some things they trust to protect them,

• study the story of Daniel and discuss the protection he received from God,

59

- explore various aspects of God's protection, and
- apply various aspects of God's protection to real-life situations.

OPENER

When everyone has arrived, have students form four groups. Assign each group a separate territory in the meeting area. Give each group one piece of cardboard, scissors, and markers. Instruct each group to create a shield from the cardboard that will protect the entire group. As they're working, have groups brainstorm various things people might rely on to protect them when they're afraid and write those items on their shields. Some examples might include locks, drugs and alcohol, television as an escape, friends, and the police.

After students have made their shields, distribute stacks of scrap paper to each group. Have each group write on the papers things they fear. For example, they might write "death," "heights," "fire," "water," "snakes," or "bad grades." Encourage students to write a lot and use a lot of paper. When students have written their ideas, have them wad their ideas into balls.

Say: **A war has just started, and you're in the middle of it! All these other groups want to take over your territory, and you have to defend yourselves. Gather your paper wads, hide behind your shields, and advance to take over another group's territory by filling the territory with as much paper as you can. Whoever has the least amount of paper in their territory when I call "time" wins. Ready? Go!**

Instruct groups to decide who will go out and try to fill other teams' areas with paper wads and who will stay and defend their territory and hide behind the shields. Allow groups time to try to take over another group's territory.

After several minutes, stop the game and evaluate which team has the least amount of paper in their territory. Declare that team the winner. Then say: **Great job taking over another territory. Now I'd like you to examine your defense against their attacks.** Have each group select four paper wads from the floor in its territory. Have groups read the paper wads and use the ideas on

BIBLE BACKGROUND

You may want to share this background information with your students to help them understand the story of Daniel.

The king Daniel dealt with in this passage eludes much description because historians aren't exactly sure who he was.

Some Bible scholars believe his real name was "Gubaru," who was originally an official in Cyrus' army and was made the king of Babylon by Cyrus. Others believe Darius was actually Cyrus himself. Cyrus was one of the key figures in the Persian Empire. He was well-known as a powerful ruler and the leader of an almost invincible army.

One of the notable events Cyrus orchestrated colors the time in which many believe this book was written. Cyrus conquered Babylon in 539 B.C. (where the Jews had been held captive since 605 B.C.). Shortly after doing so, he sent those who had been held captive back to their home countries. Cyrus was instrumental in returning the Jews back to their home.

---

their shields to think up ways they could be protected from the ideas on the papers. For example, if they read a paper that says "fire," students might suggest that they buy a fire extinguisher.

When groups are finished, have them report their ideas.

UNDERSTANDING GOD'S WORD

Say: **Sometimes we feel like we're powerless against the things we're afraid of. But when we feel like we need protection, we can rely on God to protect us.**

Have students remain in their teams. Remind students about the story of Daniel. Explain that Daniel was someone who easily could have let his fears rule over his desire to honor God—but he didn't. Daniel faced the threat of death with the confidence that God could protect him. Have each group choose a reader to read aloud Daniel 6:1-28 to the group. Then ask each group to brainstorm three words that describe Daniel's confidence and then share their words with the other groups.

After groups have shared, ask the following questions, giving groups time to discuss each one:

• **Why would the king allow a tried-and-true friend of his to be placed in the lions' den?**

• **Do you think God protected Daniel to save Daniel, or to send a message to the king? Explain.**

• **How do you think Daniel reacted when the lions didn't attack?**

• **Are there times when God chooses not to protect us? Explain.**

• **Why would God protect people?**

After groups have discussed the questions, have them spend time talking about times they've been protected by God. Have members share how they felt being protected and how their experiences affected their view of God.

APPLYING GOD'S WORD

Say: **Sometimes it's difficult to know when God is protecting us. Other times it's abundantly clear. God's protection is understood differently by different people. Let's spend some time processing how we understand God's protection.**

Have students form three groups, and give one copy of "The Power of Protection" handout (p. 64) to each group. Assign each group one of the situations on the handout. Instruct each group to read its situation and answer the questions associated with it. After a few minutes, have groups share their situations and answers. After each group presents, ask the two other groups if they have any more ideas to add. Then ask:

• How can you know when you're receiving God's protection?

• What compels God to protect us?

• Are there people God doesn't protect? If so, who might those people be?

• What should our response to God be when we know that God's protecting us?

• What should our response be when we feel God isn't protecting us?

WORSHIP TIME

Have students form four groups, and give each group a copy of "The Worship of Protection" handout (p. 65) and a pen or pencil. Have groups work through their handouts. When all groups are finished, gather groups together in the center of your meeting room and have each group present what it created in the worship experience.

CLOSING

Gather groups in a circle around a cross or a drawing of a cross on newsprint. Say: **Ultimately, it's God's love that protects us. It was God's love that compelled him to protect Daniel. In the time that has passed between Daniel and us, nothing about God's love has changed. God loves us just as much as he loved**

BIBLE BACKGROUND

You may want to share this background information with your students to help them understand the story of Daniel.

Basically, the way a lions' den worked was pretty simple. The lions lived in the room next to a cavern. When someone was scheduled to be executed, the stone on top of the larger room would be removed and the doomed person would be tossed in. Because there were no windows, escape was impossible.

Daniel. And God longs for us to depend on his protection.

Distribute one index card to each student. Have each person write one specific way he or she feels the need for protection. When students are finished, have them fold their cards and tape them to the cross. Then close the session in prayer, asking God to protect everyone.

The Power of Protection

1 Situation

Bill walks alone to school every day. And every day he's becoming more and more concerned about the guys who stand on the corner. At first the guys didn't say anything. But the other day they followed him for a while and began shouting at him. Today it got worse. They began following him, and when Bill saw them behind him, he began to run. They chased him until they had him cornered on a side street. Then they threw rocks at him and threatened him.

Bill has just told you about this. And he wants to know what you think.

• How can you help Bill understand God's protection?

• Should Bill be as bold as Daniel? Explain.

• What would you counsel Bill to do next?

2 Situation

It's been three years since the crash on Highway 189. Jenny still feels like everything is her fault.

Jenny and three friends had set out for a well-planned double date. The rain hadn't deterred the four teenagers from heading for the bowling alley. Jenny had been excited about the evening and glad to be with her friends. Halfway to the bowling alley, Phil lost control and sent the car into a collision course with a semi. The next morning, Jenny was the only one alive.

It was hard for her to deal with the death of her friends, but the pain has decreased over time. Now she's facing another struggle. Some people have told her that the only reason she's alive is because she's a Christian and the others weren't. God took the three other people because they didn't believe in him.

Jenny doesn't know what to believe. But she's sure she needs to think the whole thing over.

• If God protects us, why does he allow us to be harmed?

• Why didn't God let Daniel die in the lions' den? Why does God allow some people to die?

• What should you say to Jenny to comfort her?

3 Situation

Phil can't believe the conversation he just had. It all began over something he did at lunch.

Phil usually sits with the yearbook staff at lunch and talks about life. But today he missed his normal lunch time and had to catch a quick meal between classes. He got his food, sat down, and began to pray. About halfway through his prayer he heard, "What are you doing?"

Phil looked up, startled. "What do you mean? I'm praying for my food." Phil noticed it was Steve. Steve had a history of doing things like this to people who identified themselves as Christians in the school.

"Oh! You're one of those Christian people. I really can't stand people like you." It began with that and continued with an onslaught of religious insults and swearing. Phil couldn't believe what he was hearing. He took a bite of food and tried to ignore the incident.

"Hey, you jerk, you can't ignore me. What gives you the right to pray for your food in this school anyway?" A teacher noticed what Steve was doing and quickly escorted him to the principal's office. Phil just sat there, completely taken aback.

• How might God protect Phil? Explain.

• How would you help Phil?

• How is this situation like the one Daniel faced?

• Based on what you know about Daniel's life, what should Phil do?

The Worship of Protection

ASKING:
Write a request for help from someone who strongly desires God's protection. You might want to create a situation where someone feels like he or she is in certain danger and turns to God for help. Be sure to include in the request a detailed list of why this person feels a need for God's protection.

Receiving
Create a pantomime of someone receiving God's protection. For the subject of your mime, consider creating a modern-day situation like Daniel's.

Perspective:
Draw a picture of God's view of protection. Consider the following ideas: God protecting us like a parent, God protecting us like a police officer, God protecting us like a big brother. Look at the need for protection from one of those perspectives.

Thanks!
Write a poem that thanks God for protection. You might want to use the person from the "Receiving" step above. Look at the protection that person received and create a response that person might have.

A Fish Story

BIBLE CHARACTER: JONAH

SCRIPTURE: Jonah 1–4

THEME:
God teaches us.

SUPPLIES:
You'll need photocopies of the "Walking in Jonah's Shoes" handout (p. 72), construction paper, pens or pencils, sheets of 1x½-inch self-stick labels (two sheets per person), Bibles, index cards, and an offering plate or basket.

PREPARATION

Before the session, make one photocopy of the "Walking in Jonah's Shoes" handout (p. 72) for each person.

Familiarize yourself with the story of Jonah. Then read the entire session outline. Make sure all the activities fit your group, and make any necessary changes.

OVERVIEW

Through God's work in Jonah's life, we can see a special picture of God's grace. Disobedient Jonah fought hard against God. But God didn't reject him. Instead, God used Jonah's failures to teach and strengthen him. In the same way, God uses our failures to help us find meaning in our lives. In this session students will

• be reminded of the special strengths and gifts God has given them,

• understand that God gives us opportunities to learn from our mistakes,

• identify areas in their own lives that God has used to teach and strengthen them,

• identify areas in their lives where they're resisting God's will and reflect on how God might use the opportunity to deepen their Christian faith, and

• recognize that the lessons of the Bible are timeless and applicable today.

OPENER

Have participants form groups of three. Give each person a sheet of construction paper, a pen or pencil, and two sheets of self-stick labels. Instruct each participant to write his or her name in the middle of the construction paper.

Say: **We don't often take the opportunity to reflect on the strengths God has given us. In this activity we're going to point out some of the strengths and talents we see in each other. One person in your group will spend two or three minutes telling about his or her life. This should include childhood memories, activities at school, family events, and so forth. While one person is telling his or her story, the other two in the group are to listen closely and write words on the labels that describe the strengths and talents they notice in the person's life.**

For example, if someone tells about taking care of a younger brother and teaching him to tie his shoes, the other two might write words such as "caretaker," "teacher," "caring," or "loving."

Continue writing strengths while the person tells about his or her life. When the first person finishes, the other two should stick their labels to the first person's sheet of construction paper. Proceed in the same manner with the second person telling his or her story while the other two make note of obvious strengths and talents. Continue also with the third person until everyone is finished. Try to stick to two or three minutes per person.

When all groups have finished this affirming activity, ask:

• **What did you learn about yourself in this activity?**

• **How were you impacted by the strengths and talents recognized by the other two?**

> ## TIP
> Having more than three participants per group will extend the length of this activity significantly.

UNDERSTANDING GOD'S WORD

Say: **It's no accident that each of us has different strengths. The Bible reminds us that God carefully created us to be special.** Ask a volunteer to read Psalm 139:13-16 aloud to the group.

Say: **God purposely made us with unique talents, and at different times in our lives God will call on us to use our strengths to serve him.**

There are many stories in the Bible of God calling people to use their talents. One of the most interesting stories is that of Jonah. God called Jonah to use his gift of preaching among the sinful people in a city called Nineveh. But Jonah resisted God's call and tried to flee from the mission. What followed was an interesting series of events that God used to teach Jonah several lessons. In the same way, God often uses the events of our lives to teach us and help us grow stronger in our Christian faith.

Ask a volunteer to summarize the story of Jonah for the class. If no one is able or willing, provide a brief overview of the events. Then ask:

• **Why do you think Jonah disobeyed God?**

• **Which events in the life of Jonah let us know that God didn't give up on him?**

Have teenagers form four somewhat equal groups. Give each participant a photocopy of the "Walking in Jonah's Shoes" handout. Assign each group a segment of the handout and the corresponding chapter of the book of Jonah.

Instruct each group to follow the instructions on the handout. After approximately fifteen minutes, or when groups have completed their discussions, call everyone back together. Have a spokesperson from each group report this information in order of the group's assigned chapter:

• **Give a brief summary of the chapter.**

• **How did God use the opportunity to teach Jonah about his relationship with God?**

• **What advice would your group give Jonah?**

• **What was your group's theme song for the chapter?**

BIBLE BACKGROUND

You may want to share this background information with your students to help them understand the story of Jonah.

It's somewhat understandable that Jonah didn't want to go preach in Nineveh, a wicked city in Assyria. Jonah was an Israelite, and the Israelites feared and hated the Assyrians. Jonah was reluctant to share God's love and mercy with these people who actually were the enemies of the Israelites.

When all groups have finished their reports, say: **Jonah's story teaches us a lot about ourselves and God. But most important, it teaches us that God uses even our unchristian attitudes to teach us about ourselves and about our relationship with God.**

Ask:

• **What is the most important lesson you think Jonah learned about God from his experiences?**

• **What's the most important lesson you've learned about God during your own personal experiences so far?**

APPLYING GOD'S WORD

Instruct students to remain in their four groups and to use the main idea from their assigned Jonah chapters to create modern-day role plays. For example, for the chapter about Jonah avoiding God, a group might create a modern-day role-play of a student who avoids making friends with a new student, even though he or she is aware of the Christian responsibility to reach out to others in friendship.

Say: **Each role-play should be only two or three minutes in length and can use as few or as many of the participants in your group as you choose. You have approximately two minutes to create the role-play.**

After groups have had an opportunity to prepare, have groups take turns making their presentations to the whole group. After each presentation, ask: **How could God use this event to teach us about our relationships with God and others?**

WORSHIP TIME

Give each person an index card and a pen or pencil. Say: **God called Jonah to go on a mission to Nineveh to do something Jonah really didn't want to do. We can understand Jonah's feelings. Sometimes we know God wants us to do something but, like Jonah, we feel uncomfortable, scared, or inadequate.**

Take a moment to reflect on your own life. What can you identify as your "Nineveh," or, in other words, something you're trying

to avoid in your life right now? a difficult person? a problem at school? a family situation? a particular issue of sin in your life? a closer relationship with God? or something else? Use your index card to record what you identify as your personal Nineveh. No one will see what you write—this is just between you and God.

Pause for a minute or two to allow teenagers to reflect. Then continue:

Take a minute now to reflect on how you think God will use this situation to teach you about your relationship with him. Record your thoughts on your card.

Again, pause for a minute or two.

Say: **We're going to quietly take up an offering now. As we do, present your card as a special offering, committing to God to learn from God through your Nineveh. Be assured that these cards will be destroyed without anyone reading them. As the offering is taken, silently reflect and pray about your Nineveh. Remember, this is a time of worship.**

After the offering has been taken, pray that God will use the events in the teenagers' lives to teach them to be stronger Christians.

CLOSING

Instruct everyone to find a partner. When pairs are together, say: **Uh oh! You were so interested in Jonah's story that you decided to take a boat trip and try to retrace the journey he took across the sea when he was running from God. Everything was going great until the cook on the ship served some really bad fish. After the meal, the doctor informed you that the fish were poisonous and you now have only one year to live.** Share with your partner your answers to these questions:

• **Would having only a year left make it easier or more difficult to overcome your personal Nineveh? Why?**

• **What is something you think God would want you to accomplish if you had only one year to live?**

Say: **In our study of Jonah, we learned that even though Jonah fought hard against God, God didn't reject him. Instead**

BIBLE BACKGROUND

You may want to share this background information with your students to help them understand the story of Jonah.

For some people, the story of Jonah is one of the most difficult Bible stories to believe because it seems so unlikely that a man could have been swallowed by a large fish and live for three days. As a result, some people suggest the story of Jonah is an allegory, or a symbolical story, and not literal or historical.

There are, however, certain species of whales and sharks that can actually swallow a person whole. In addition, there has been at least one real-life story about a person being swallowed by a whale and surviving the experience.

God used Jonah's failures to teach and strengthen him. Sometimes, like Jonah, we fail by avoiding something we know we should do until it's too late. Let us now pray and commit ourselves to respond to God's teaching in our lives.

Close the session with prayer.

Walking in Jonah's Shoes

Instructions: Ask a volunteer in your group to read your assigned chapter aloud, or have several readers take turns. Then respond to the questions listed beneath your chapter. Each group should pick a spokesperson who will be responsible for summarizing the group's discussion and presenting it to the entire group. Assign someone in the group to take a few notes about the results of your discussion. Assign one person in your group to lead the discussion.

Dissatisfaction with God's outcome *(Chapter 4)*

Obeying God *(Chapter 3)*

Bargaining with God *(Chapter 2)*

Running from God *(Chapter 1)*

The four stages of Jonah's journey

GROUP 1 (Running from God)
Read chapter 1.

- What do you think was going through Jonah's mind when he was running from God?
- How did God use this opportunity to teach Jonah about his relationship with God?
- Take turns telling about a time in your life when you avoided doing something you believed God wanted you to do.
- As you look back on that event, how did God use the opportunity to teach you something about yourself and your relationship with God?
- Looking at the events of this chapter, if you could give some advice to Jonah, what would it be, and why?
- After his own experiences, if Jonah looked at your life right now, what advice would he give you?
- Pick a theme song (any song you know) that describes this chapter.

GROUP 2 (Bargaining wth God)
Read chapter 2.

- What do you think was going through Jonah's mind as he was inside the fish?
- How did God use this opportunity to teach Jonah about his relationship with God?
- Take turns telling about a time in your life when you were in need of help and tried to bargain with God.
- As you look back on that event, how did God use the opportunity to teach you something about yourself and your relationship with God?
- Looking at the events of this chapter, if you could give some advice to Jonah, what would it be, and why?
- If Jonah looked at your life right now, what advice would he give you?
- Pick a theme song (any song you know) that describes this chapter.

GROUP 3 (Obeying God)
Read chapter 3.

- What do you think was going through Jonah's mind when he finally decided to obey God?
- How did God use this opportunity to teach Jonah about his relationship with God?
- Take turns telling about a time in your life when you did something you knew God wanted you to do.
- As you look back on the event, how did God use the opportunity to teach you something about yourself and your relationship with God?
- Looking at the events of this chapter, if you could give some advice to Jonah, what would it be, and why?
- After his own experiences, if Jonah looked at your life right now, what advice would he give you?
- Pick a theme song (any song you know) that describes this chapter.

GROUP 4 (Dissatisfaction with God's outcome)
Read chapter 4.

- What do you think was going through Jonah's mind when he became displeased with the outcome of God's work?
- How did God use the opportunity to teach Jonah about his relationship with God?
- Take turns telling about a time in your life when you were dissatisfied or unhappy with God.
- As you look back at the event, how did God use the opportunity to teach you something about yourself and your relationship with God?
- Looking at the events of this chapter, if you could give some advice to Jonah, what would it be, and why?
- After his own experiences, if Jonah looked at your life right now, what advice would he give you?
- Pick a theme song (any song you know) that describes this chapter.

Permission to photocopy this handout from *Living Beyond Belief* granted for local church use. Copyright © Group Publishing, Inc., P.O. Box 481, Loveland, CO 80539.

Canceled Debts

A SINFUL WOMAN

BIBLE CHARACTER:

SCRIPTURE: Luke 7:36-50

THEME:
God forgives us.

SUPPLIES:
You'll need photocopies of the "Prayer of Confession" handout (p. 80), paper, pens or pencils, balloons, markers, string, scissors, Bibles, newsprint, and tape.

PREPARATION

Before the session, make one photocopy of the "Prayer of Confession" handout (p. 80) for each student.

Study Luke 7:36-50. Then read the entire session outline. Make sure all the activities fit your group, and make any necessary changes.

OVERVIEW

This session teaches students about a sinful woman's experience with Jesus. It reminds students that God wants to forgive them no matter how they've sinned. Students will
- calculate the debts they owe,
- study Jesus' forgiveness of a sinful woman,

- replicate the sinful woman's repentant attitude in their own lives,
- confess their sins, and
- experience the peace of forgiveness.

OPENER

Distribute paper and pens or pencils, and have teenagers form pairs. Ask pairs to discuss what a debt is and what kinds of debts they owe to others. After a few minutes of discussion, ask volunteers to share their definitions of the word "debt" and what kinds of debts they owe. Then say: **It's time to see how your debts have been adding up. Think of everything you can that you owe to others, whether you owe money, material things, favors, or even gratitude. Write down each debt on your paper, and remember to include every debt you can think of.**

When students have finished listing their debts, ask them to assign a dollar amount to each debt and then add up their debts. Encourage students to have fun with this portion of the activity; if a debt of gratitude is priceless, they can assign it an astronomical dollar amount.

Distribute balloons, markers, and two-foot lengths of string, and have each person blow up and tie off a balloon. Then have each student write on a balloon a sentence that includes his or her name and total debt—"Kim owes seven billion dollars," for example. Finally, have students use string to tie their balloons around their wrists.

When everyone has finished, ask volunteers to explain the amount of debt they owe. Ask:

- **Are you surprised by what you owe? Why or why not?**
- **What is it like to be indebted to others?**
- **Do you have debts you will never be able to pay? Explain.**
- **How is sin like debt?**
- **Can we ever do anything to reduce the debt of our sin? Explain.**

Say: **Our debt of sin can feel a lot like an expanding balloon. We feel like we owe more and more, but we can't sufficiently pay** for our debt of sin. Today we're going to learn how God dealt with one woman's debt of sin, and that'll help us understand how he deals with our debt of sin too.

Have teenagers wear their balloons until they receive further instructions. If a person's balloon pops during the session, provide a new one for him or her to tie around a wrist.

UNDERSTANDING GOD'S WORD

Have students form groups of four, and distribute newsprint and markers. Ask groups to read Luke 7:36-50 and then discuss the following questions:

• **How do you think the woman felt before she entered the house? Why?**

• **How was the woman's sin like debt?**

• **How did the woman feel about her debt?**

Have the groups draw on the top third of their pieces of newsprint a picture of the woman to represent the state she was in before she entered the house and met Jesus. Explain that groups may draw symbolic pictures or realistic pictures. For example, a group could draw a woman carrying a large rock on her shoulders to show the burden she carried, or an outline of a woman to represent the emptiness the woman felt.

Give the groups about five minutes to discuss and draw their pictures. Then ask each group's members to explain the picture they drew.

Afterward, have groups read Luke 7:36-50 again and discuss the following questions:

• **How do you think the woman felt as she left the house? Why?**

• **How did Jesus affect the woman's life?**

Have the groups draw on the bottom third of their pieces of newsprint a picture of the woman to represent the state she was in after she left the house. Again, explain that groups may draw symbolic or realistic pictures. For example, a group could draw a

---

BIBLE BACKGROUND

You may want to share this background information with your students to help them understand the story of the sinful woman in Luke 7.

In Jesus' time, highly respected people were afforded special treatment as guests in people's homes. Servants would wash and dry the guest's feet, which undoubtedly would be dirty after a journey on dusty streets.

woman with a rock removed from her shoulders to show that Jesus removed her burden, or an outline of a woman with facial features and a heart drawn in to show the fullness of love the woman received from Jesus.

Give the groups about five minutes to discuss and draw their pictures. Then ask each group's members to explain the picture they drew.

Afterward, have groups read Luke 7:36-50 one more time and discuss these questions:

• **What different emotions did the woman express during her time in Jesus' presence?**

• **How did the woman show faith?**

• **What did the differences between Simon's actions and the sinful woman's actions say about how they felt about Jesus?**

• **What do Jesus' actions toward Simon and the sinful woman teach you about the debt of sin?**

Have the groups draw on their newsprint pieces a road connecting the two pictures. On the right side of the road, have the groups draw road signs that illustrate the convictions or attitudes the woman expressed from the time she entered the house until she left the house. On the left side of the road, have the groups draw road signs that illustrate what Jesus did for the woman from the time she entered the house until she left the house. Finally, have groups create titles for their newsprint posters to express what their posters illustrate.

After about five minutes, have each group tape its newsprint poster to a wall and explain the road signs and title. After every group has presented its poster, have groups discuss these questions:

• **How was the difference between Simon's response to Jesus and the woman's response to Jesus significant?**

• **How did the woman show her faith?**

• **What was the woman's attitude toward her debt of sin?**

• **What could the woman herself do about her debt of sin?**

• **What did Jesus do about the woman's debt of sin?**

• **What does this event teach you about your own debt? about forgiveness?**

BIBLE BACKGROUND

You may want to share this background information with your students to help them understand the story of the sinful woman in Luke 7.

Anointing, or pouring oil on yourself, was seen as a sign of luxury or festivity in biblical times. New kings were anointed with oil as a sign of power and authority being passed to them, as David was anointed king of Israel by the prophet Samuel (1 Samuel 16). People and objects also were anointed with oil to signify that they were set apart as holy, as the newly built tabernacle and its furnishings were anointed (Exodus 40). When the sinful woman of Luke 7 poured aromatic oils on Jesus' feet, she symbolically recognized his power, authority, and holiness.

Say: **A woman who had led a sinful life heard about Jesus, met him, and simply wept from the debt of sin she carried and from the love and forgiveness Jesus offered. By her actions and Jesus' words about her, we know this woman recognized Jesus' holiness and authority. And Jesus responded to this sinful woman by granting her lasting peace through forgiveness. It's one of the most touching stories in the Bible—and one of the most hopeful for all of us because we all carry a debt of sin.**

APPLYING GOD'S WORD

Ask:

• **When have you felt like the woman did before she entered the house? after she left the house?**

• **Do you think any debt of sin is too large for Jesus to forgive? Explain.**

• **What's the difference between the role you play and the role God plays in the cancellation of your debt of sin?**

Have students remain in their groups of four, and distribute paper and pens or pencils. Have groups examine the posters from the previous activity, paying special attention to the road signs illustrating the woman's attitudes. Have each group list four attitudes that can demonstrate that a person is ready for forgiveness—repentance, humility, love, and faith, for example. Be sure to emphasize that although these attitudes may demonstrate that a person is ready for forgiveness, our forgiveness is not earned through our actions but is granted through God's grace.

Ask group members to think about something for which they need to experience God's forgiveness and then to summarize their situations for each other, sharing only what makes them comfortable. For example, someone could either tell the whole story about an argument he or she had with a teacher or simply say he or she needs God's forgiveness for anger.

After each person has shared a situation, have group members help each other determine how the attitudes of forgiveness they listed may look in that person's life. For example, just as the woman in the Scripture wept, which demonstrated her repentance, how

77

would the student demonstrate repentance? Just as the woman wiped her tears off Jesus' feet, which demonstrated her humility, how would the student demonstrate humility? Have groups continue the process until each group member has thought about what those attitudes may look like in his or her own life. Then have groups discuss these questions:

• When have you experienced God's forgiveness?

• How is forgiveness like a cancellation of debt?

• What difference does forgiveness make in your life today? in your future?

• How does it feel to have a debt of sin canceled?

Say: **Before we're forgiven, we carry around a load of debt kind of like the balloons you're carrying around today. Sin gets in our way, constantly holding us back with tugging reminders that it's still there. Jesus changes our lives by canceling that debt of sin just as he canceled the woman's debt of sin. Jesus sets us free.**

WORSHIP TIME

Give everyone a photocopy of the "Prayer of Confession" handout (p. 80). Explain that students will walk around the room together and, at each corner, will follow the directions on the handout and read the prayer silently to God if they choose to. Lead the group to one corner, and begin.

Afterward, ask:

• What was it like to confess your sins and ask for forgiveness?

• How does it feel to have the balloon off your wrist?

• How is that like the way it feels to have your debt of sin canceled?

CLOSING

Say: **The last words Jesus said to the woman in the story we learned about today were "go in peace."** Ask:

• How does forgiveness bring peace?

Explain that to contrast the debt of sin and the peace of forgiveness, everyone will stomp on the balloons until they're popped. Also explain that when the last balloon is popped, everyone should sit down and be silent.

Have students start stomping on the balloons. When the last balloon has been popped, lead students in sitting down. Encourage teenagers to sit silently for a minute or two and thank God for the peace of forgiveness.

Prayer of Confession

CORNER ONE

Kneel on the floor and pray, "Dear God, I sometimes forget or ignore that you are perfect and holy. When I sin, it's as if I'm telling you that I know better than you. I realize that I don't know better than you and that I should choose to do things your way every time."

CORNER TWO

Stand with your head bowed and pray, "God, I'm sorry for my sin. I want to tell you now about the things I've done for which I need your forgiveness." Pray silently, expressing to God the things you've done for which you need God's forgiveness.

CORNER THREE

Stand with one hand raised, and pray, "God, I love you for everything you are and everything you do for me. It's amazing that I can come to you with my sin and that you still accept me and love me anyway."

CORNER FOUR

Take the balloon off your wrist, put it in a pile with everyone else's balloons, and pray, "Thank you for forgiving me, God. Thank you for loving me and canceling my debt of sin again and again. Just as the woman in the story was grateful, I'm grateful to you for your forgiveness."

Kneel Down

BIBLE CHARACTER: Martha

SCRIPTURE: Luke 10:38-42

THEME:
God wants us to know him.

SUPPLIES:
You'll need photocopies of the "Best Friends Info Sheet" handout (p. 85) and the "Characteristics of God" handout (p. 86), pens or pencils, enough costume elements and props (such as hats, funny clothes, an umbrella, a note pad, a small plant, a piece of fruit) for each person to have one, Bibles, a coin, a watch with a second hand, a dry-erase board or newsprint and a marker, and index cards.

PREPARATION

Before the session, make one photocopy of the "Best Friends Info Sheet" (p. 85) handout and the "Characteristics of God" handout (p. 86) for each person.

Study Luke 10:38-42. Then read the entire session outline. Make sure all the activities fit your group, and make any necessary changes.

OVERVIEW

This study teaches students that God wants us to know him. God values the time we spend learning about him and from him. Students will

- become aware of what it means to know someone,
- study Martha's experience with Jesus,
- learn that Jesus wants to spend time with us, and
- commit to taking a step to know God better.

BIBLE BACKGROUND

You may want to share this background information with the students to help them gain insight into the story of Martha.

Jesus' time was both in great demand by his followers and of little value to the many people who were hostile to his existence. It's amazing that such a popular man would go out of his way to honor two women, especially in a male-dominated society. Mary and Martha were close to Jesus. Jesus loved their family (John 11:5) and valued spending time with individual people, not just the masses.

On the other hand, many people despised Jesus and wanted to kill him. It was dangerous for Mary and Martha to invite Jesus into their home (John 12:10-11). They ran the risk of being rejected by their own people or even killed for associating with him. But Mary and Martha wanted to take the risk.

It's possible that Martha was a widow, which made her head of the household

continued on page 83

OPENER

Give each person a "Best Friends Info Sheet" handout and a pen or pencil, and instruct students to answer the questions on the handout. Then instruct each person to create a commercial that "sells" his or her friend to the rest of the group.

Give each person a prop and a costume element. Allow students a few minutes to prepare their commercials before they perform. If you have more than eight people in your group, you may want to have students form groups of four or five and perform their commercials only for the people in their group.

UNDERSTANDING GOD'S WORD

Say: **Just as we know the likes, dislikes, and characteristics of our closest friends, we can continue to grow in our relationship with God and know God's likes, dislikes, and characteristics. We can learn a lot about how to get close to God by observing how we become close to people here on earth. True intimacy happens between people and between God and us when we allow ourselves to be truly known. God wants us to take time to get to know him. Today we're going to examine a story about two of Jesus' closest friends.** Have one student read Luke 10:38-42 aloud.

Tell students they're going to engage in a debate. Have students form two teams, and send each team to one side of the meeting area. Assign one group Martha and the other side Mary. Tell the Martha team they must support the idea that Jesus was too harsh with Martha. Tell the Mary side to support the opinion that Jesus wasn't too harsh with Martha. Be sure everyone knows there will be no real winner in this debate; this is just for fun.

Give teams several minutes to discuss their arguments and to develop five points to support their cases. When each team is ready, flip a coin to decide which team will go first. Only one team can speak at a time, for sixty seconds each time. Allow each team to take five turns speaking. Control the debate by encouraging different people to speak and allowing only one person to speak

continued from page 82

(Henry Matthew, *The NIV Matthew Henry Commentary in One Volume*). As head of the house, it would have been her duty to watch over the affairs of the house. Therefore Martha would have felt a great responsibility to be hospitable to Jesus.

at a time. After the debate, ask any of the following questions that weren't answered in the debate:

• **Why do you think Jesus came to visit Mary and Martha? What was his greatest need?**

• **Why do you think Martha was so eager to make preparations for Jesus?**

• **Why do you think Mary behaved differently?**

• **What did Mary have to sacrifice in order to get to know Jesus better?**

• **Why do you think Jesus said Martha's name twice?**

• **When would it be better to give the way Martha was giving?**

APPLYING GOD'S WORD

Ask students to sit quietly for a few moments and think about their own lives. Say: **Think about your relationship with God. Are you more like Mary or more like Martha? Do you take time to talk with God and listen to God, or are you too busy doing things for God?** Ask:

• **What does it mean to know God?**

• **What are ways you can get to know God better?**

• **What changes do you need to make in your life so you'll have more time to spend with God?**

Encourage youth to spread out and get comfortable. Ask students to spend the next few minutes in silence before God. Say: **Take advantage of the next few minutes to sit at Jesus' feet the way Mary did. You may want to spend this time in silent prayer, or you may want to just listen to God and enjoy being in his presence.**

After a few minutes, gather everyone back together for a time of worship.

WORSHIP TIME

Give each student a "Characteristics of God" handout. Say: **As a way to worship God, I'd like each person to pick one of the characteristics on this handout and explain why that characteristic is personally important to you. As you share, give a specific example**

83

of when you've seen God show that characteristic in your life. For example, perhaps God's faithfulness is important to you because your parents are divorced and you rarely see your dad. Maybe it's comforting to know that God is always faithful to listen to you and help you. Perhaps when you're lonely, God shows you his faithfulness through your friends.

You may want to share your own story first as an example for youth.

CLOSING

Say: **The God of the universe wants to spend time with you. God wants you to feel his amazing love. Let's think of some specific ways we can get to know God better over the next week.**

Ask students to name specific ways to get to know God better. As they call out ideas, write their answers on a dry-erase board or a piece of newsprint. Then give each person an index card and say: **I'd like you to read through the ideas we listed and pick one you can do over the next week. If you're ready to commit to getting to know God better this week, write that idea on your index card as a reminder. When you get home, put this card in a place where it will help you remember to get to know God better this week.**

Close in prayer, asking God to help students follow through on their commitments.

best friends
info sheet

❥ Who is one of your closest friends?

❥ What's your friend's favorite color?

❥ What's your friend's favorite thing to do?

❥ What are some things that really bother this person?

❥ What are your friend's greatest strengths?

❥ What three words best describe your friend's personality?

❥ What are the benefits of being friends with this person?

❥ How did you become close friends with this person?

Characteristics of God

All-powerful
(Genesis 18:14; Matthew 19:26)

Everywhere
(Psalm 139:7-10)

All-knowing
(Proverbs 5:21)

Unchanging
(Numbers 23:19; James 1:17)

In complete control
(Ephesians 1:11)

Eternal
(Exodus 3:14; Psalm 90:1-2)

Just
(Zephaniah 3:17-20)

Relational
(Psalm 23)

Gracious
(Psalms 103:8; 116:5; Lamentations 3:21-23)

Merciful
(Romans 5:6-11)

Holy
(Leviticus 11:44-45)

Love
(1 John 4:7-10)

Truth
(John 14:6)

Come Down From Your Tree

BIBLE CHARACTER: ZACCHAEUS

SCRIPTURE: Luke 19:1-10

THEME:
God changes us.

SUPPLIES:
You'll need Bibles, photocopies of the "Criminal Bios" handout (p. 91), photocopies of the "Draw Your Partner" handout (p. 92), books and encyclopedias with information about ants, pens or pencils, a dry-erase board or newsprint and a marker, crayons or markers, worship music, a cassette or CD player, a large bottle, vinegar, and baking soda.

PREPARATION

Before the session, make one photocopy of the "Criminal Bios" handout (p. 91) and the "Draw Your Partner" handout (p. 92) for each person. Do a trial run on the vinegar and baking soda experiment in the Closing. Fill the bottle halfway with vinegar, and use about a tablespoon of baking soda, or enough to create foam.

Study Luke 19:1-10. Then read the entire session outline. Make sure all the activities fit your group, and make any necessary changes.

OVERVIEW

This study teaches students that God wants to change us and will when we allow him to. God will change our hearts, our lifestyles, and our eternal destinations. Students will
- become aware of their personal need to change,
- study the way Jesus entered Zacchaeus' life and changed him,
- ask God to change them in specific ways, and
- experience an object lesson on how God changes people.

BIBLE BACKGROUND

You may want to share this background information with the students to help them gain insight into the story of Zacchaeus.

Zacchaeus was a chief tax collector, which meant he was in charge of a large group of tax collectors. He was a leader with influence and power. He could have used his influence to either help people or bring them harm. Zacchaeus was a corrupt man because in addition to collecting taxes, he collected more than was needed and pocketed the leftover. He was disliked because he cheated his own people in order to be rich. In fact, Zacchaeus was so hated, some people believe he ran ahead of the crowd in order to avoid them.

The Scriptures say Zacchaeus welcomed Jesus gladly into his home. He was full of joy to serve Jesus. It's significant that Zacchaeus wanted Jesus to come to his home. Since he was so corrupt, it's surprising that he wanted to welcome into his home someone who would strongly disagree with his lifestyle. His willingness to spend time with Jesus may

continued on page 89

OPENER

Give each person a "Criminal Bios" handout, and have students form groups of about four people. In their groups, have teenagers read the handout and discuss the questions.

UNDERSTANDING GOD'S WORD

Say: **In order for God to change us, we need to accept that there are areas in our lives that need to be changed. At times we can be so focused on how sinful someone else is that we don't realize we're just as sinful. Some of our sins may not cause as much damage or may not be as obvious as another person's sin, but we're equally capable of hurting people. We need to understand God's primary role in sending Jesus to us.**

Ask two volunteers to read Luke 19:1-10 aloud, each person reading five verses.

In their groups, have students answer the following questions:
- **Why did Zacchaeus want to see Jesus?**
- **What do you think started the change in Zacchaeus?**
- **Why do you think Jesus chose to go to the house of Zacchaeus?**
- **Why do you think Zacchaeus gave half his possessions to the poor?**
- **How did God change Zacchaeus?**
- **Why do you think God would want to change people if he created them in the first place?**
- **What hinders people from being changed by God?**

APPLYING GOD'S WORD

Say: **Proverbs 6:6 says, "Go to the ant, you sluggard; consider its ways and be wise!"** Observing nature is a great way to learn some of God's principles that can apply to us.

Have students form as many groups as you have books and encyclopedias about ants. Give each group one book or encyclopedia, and

continued from page 88

have been an indication of his willingness to believe in Jesus.

The crowds responded to Jesus' actions with disapproval. This shows their complete lack of humility and lack of understanding of their own sinfulness. They completely misunderstood why Jesus existed. They were unwilling to be changed by God.

BIBLE BACKGROUND

You may want to share this background information with the students to help them gain insight into the story of Zacchaeus.

Once Zacchaeus' heart started to change, he no longer could live a corrupt lifestyle. He wanted to pay back the people he had cheated. According to Jewish law (Exodus 22:1), payback was four times the amount of the stolen item.

Zacchaeus' actions followed his faith. When God changes us, he changes both our hearts and our actions. Zacchaeus wanted to change not because he feared being punished for stealing, but because God had softened his heart and given him a new perspective.

ask groups to do some research on the qualities and habits of ants.

After five to ten minutes, ask groups to call out qualities of ants. As students share ants' qualities, list their answers on a dry-erase board or a piece of newsprint. Then ask:

• **Why do you think the book of Proverbs recommends that we look at ants as examples to follow?**

• **What is one way you're like an ant in your character?**

• **What is one way you would like to be like an ant in your character?**

Say: **Proverbs also tells us that a wise person accepts correction. It's very important to have a humble and willing attitude when it comes to being changed by God. God never forces himself on us. Instead, he makes us more like Christ if we are willing to be changed.**

WORSHIP TIME

Have youth form pairs, and give each person a "Draw Your Partner" handout, a pen or pencil, and crayons or markers. While students are working, play some worship music. After partners answer the questions on the handout, have them share their answers with each other and then have each person draw his or her partner based on the partner's answers. Have students draw their partners as if the changes have already taken place.

For example, a student may share that she feels God wants her to be more generous with her possessions; then the picture would include her being generous in some way. Encourage students to be creative. After several minutes, gather the group back together and allow a few students to share their drawings.

Lead students in a prayer of dedication for their pictures. Pray aloud that students will grow to resemble the pictures their partners drew for them. Then ask the students to pray aloud or silently that God will make them more like the people their partners drew. Encourage them to pray for the specific characteristics represented in the pictures.

CLOSING

After the prayer time, pour vinegar into a large bottle until the bottle is about half full. Then pour about a tablespoon of baking soda into the bottle. The vinegar will transform and become foam. Say: **We're like the vinegar in this bottle, and God is like the baking soda. When God enters our lives, we're transformed. Let's be willing to change and depend on God to change us. As you grow to love God more, you'll be amazed at the change that will happen in your life.**

Criminal Bios

CRIMINAL 1

Every week, the worship team in Peter's youth group passed around baskets to collect money. They usually gave the money to an organization that helped poor children. Every Sunday after the service, the worship team counted the money and put it in an envelope to give to the children.

One week after the money had already been counted, Teresa brought the money to the church treasurer, as always. Before she turned in the money, she decided to count the money again—twenty dollars was missing!

The same thing happened for several weeks, so Teresa started watching the money closely. One Sunday, after the money had been counted, Teresa saw Peter reach in and take some money out of the collection. After the service, the staff asked him if he had taken money out of the offering. He denied it at first, but then finally admitted to it.

CRIMINAL 2

When Steve was only fourteen, a group of guys paid him to kill another student at their school. The group of guys convinced Steve to kill the other student because he knew too much information about their wrongdoing. So Steve brutally murdered the other student.

Steve was arrested and convicted of the crime, and he's been in a juvenile detention center ever since.

CRIMINAL 3

Julie was beautiful and popular. She lived in a wealthy neighborhood and was a great volleyball player. She also was a chronic liar.

Julie would be very nice to other people and pretend she had no money. She always convinced people to buy her food. She even convinced people to pay for her volleyball uniforms and other things she wanted. She was so popular that no one caught on because she spent time with so many different people. No one could resist her charm.

Eventually, Julie's friends found out about her lies. She lost most of her friends, and she's still one of the least popular people in school.

- Would you like to have lunch with any of these people?
- Which one of these criminals is the worst? Explain.
- If your best friend became good friends with one of these people, how would you feel? How would you respond?
- Do you have anything in common with any of these people?
- How do you feel about yourself after reading these stories?

Draw Your Partner

❖ What hinders you from becoming more like Jesus?

❖ In what areas does God want to change you?

❖ What kind of person do you think God wants you to become in the next five years?

Draw your partner below, based on your partner's answers.

Permission to photocopy this handout from *Living Beyond Belief* granted for local church use. Copyright © Group Publishing, Inc., P.O. Box 481, Loveland, CO 80539.

Group Publishing, Inc.
Attention: Product Development
P.O. Box 481
Loveland, CO 80539
Fax: (970) 679-4370

Evaluation for
Living Beyond Belief

Please help Group Publishing, Inc. continue to provide innovative and useful resources for ministry. Please take a moment to fill out this evaluation and mail or fax it to us. Thanks!

• • •

1. As a whole, this book has been (circle one)

not very helpful   very helpful

1   2   3   4   5   6   7   8   9   10

2. The best things about this book:

3. Ways this book could be improved:

4. Things I will change because of this book:

5. Other books I'd like to see Group publish in the future:

6. Would you be interested in field-testing future Group products and giving us your feedback? If so, please fill in the information below:

Name _____

Church Name _____

Denomination _____ Church Size _____

Church Address _____

City _____ State _____ ZIP _____

Church Phone _____

E-mail _____

Permission to photocopy this page granted for local church use.
Copyright © Group Publishing, Inc., P.O. Box 481, Loveland, CO 80539.

core belief
Bible Study Series

Give Your Teenagers a Solid Faith Foundation That Lasts a Lifetime!

Here are the *essentials* of the Christian life—core values teenagers *must* believe to make good decisions now...and build an *unshakable* lifelong faith. Developed by youth workers like you...field-tested with *real* youth groups in *real* churches...here's the meat your kids *must* have to grow spiritually—presented in a fun, involving way!

Each 4-session **Core Belief Bible Study Series** book lets you easily...
- Lead deep, compelling, *relevant* discussions your kids won't want to miss...
- Involve teenagers in exploring life-changing truths...
- Help kids create healthy relationships with each other—and you!

Plus you'll make an *eternal difference* in the lives of your kids as you give them a solid faith foundation that stands firm on God's Word.

Here are the Core Belief Bible Study Series titles already available...

Senior High Studies

Title	ISBN
Why **Authority** Matters	0-7644-0892-5
Why **Being a Christian** Matters	0-7644-0883-6
Why **Creation** Matters	0-7644-0880-1
Why **Forgiveness** Matters	0-7644-0887-9
Why **God** Matters	0-7644-0874-7
Why **God's Justice** Matters	0-7644-0886-0
Why **Jesus Christ** Matters	0-7644-0875-5
Why **Love** Matters	0-7644-0889-5
Why **Our Families** Matter	0-7644-0894-1
Why **Personal Character** Matters	0-7644-0885-2
Why **Prayer** Matters	0-7644-0893-3
Why **Relationships** Matter	0-7644-0896-8
Why **Serving Others** Matters	0-7644-0895-X
Why **Spiritual Growth** Matters	0-7644-0884-4
Why **Suffering** Matters	0-7644-0879-8
Why **the Bible** Matters	0-7644-0882-8
Why **the Church** Matters	0-7644-0890-9
Why **the Holy Spirit** Matters	0-7644-0876-3
Why **the Last Days** Matter	0-7644-0888-7
Why **the Spiritual Realm** Matters	0-7644-0881-X
Why **Worship** Matters	0-7644-0891-7

Junior High/Middle School Studies

Title	ISBN
The Truth About **Authority**	0-7644-0868-2
The Truth About **Being a Christian**	0-7644-0859-3
The Truth About **Creation**	0-7644-0856-9
The Truth About **Developing Character**	0-7644-0861-5
The Truth About **God**	0-7644-0850-X
The Truth About **God's Justice**	0-7644-0862-3
The Truth About **Jesus Christ**	0-7644-0851-8
The Truth About **Love**	0-7644-0865-8
The Truth About **Our Families**	0-7644-0870-4
The Truth About **Prayer**	0-7644-0869-0
The Truth About **Relationships**	0-7644-0872-0
The Truth About **Serving Others**	0-7644-0871-2
The Truth About **Sin and Forgiveness**	0-7644-0863-1
The Truth About **Spiritual Growth**	0-7644-0860-7
The Truth About **Suffering**	0-7644-0855-0
The Truth About **the Bible**	0-7644-0858-5
The Truth About **the Church**	0-7644-0899-2
The Truth About **the Holy Spirit**	0-7644-0852-6
The Truth About **the Last Days**	0-7644-0864-X
The Truth About **the Spiritual Realm**	0-7644-0857-7
The Truth About **Worship**	0-7644-0867-4

Order today from your local Christian bookstore, or write:
Group Publishing, P.O. Box 485, Loveland, CO 80539.

Exciting Resources for Your Youth Ministry

All-Star Games From All-Star Youth Leaders

The ultimate game book—from the biggest names in youth ministry! All-time no-fail favorites from Wayne Rice, Les Christie, Rich Mullins, Tiger McLuen, Darrell Pearson, Dave Stone, Bart Campolo, Steve Fitzhugh, and 21 others! You get all the games you'll need for any situation. Plus, you get practical advice about how to design your own games and tricks for turning a *good* game into a *great* game!

ISBN 0-7644-2020-8

Last Impressions: Unforgettable Closings for Youth Meetings

Make the closing moments of your youth programs powerful and memorable with this collection of Group's best-ever low-prep (or no-prep!) youth meeting closings. You get over 170 favorite closings, each tied to a thought-provoking Bible passage. Great for anyone who works with teenagers!

ISBN 1-55945-629-9

The Youth Worker's Encyclopedia of Bible-Teaching Ideas

Here are the most comprehensive idea-books available for youth workers. With more than 365 creative ideas in each of these 400-page encyclopedias, there's at least one idea for every book of the Bible. You'll find ideas for retreats and overnighters...learning games...adventures...special projects...affirmations...parties...prayers...music...devotions...skits...and more!

Old Testament ISBN 1-55945-184-X
New Testament ISBN 1-55945-183-1

PointMaker™ Devotions for Youth Ministry

These 45 PointMakers™ help your teenagers discover, understand, and apply biblical principles. Use PointMakers as brief meetings on specific topics or slide them into any youth curriculum to make a lasting impression. Includes handy Scripture and topical indexes that make it quick and easy to select the perfect PointMaker for any lesson you want to teach!

ISBN 0-7644-2003-8

Order today from your local Christian bookstore, or write: Group Publishing, P.O. Box 485, Loveland, CO 80539.